i

ISBN: 978-1-958865-09-5

Miguel de Cervantes once wrote, "He preaches well that lives well...and that is all the divinity I can understand." Cervantes provides a hint at what was both the source and the summit of the life of our colleague, brother, and friend, Harold "H" Spees: an elegance enveloped in kindness that left multitudes of people and institutions better. It is to him in whose memory we dedicate this book.

The impact of H's life on people and places cannot be overstated. He was one of those rare souls that was fiercely committed to Jesus and fully ecumenical, deadly serious with an infectious sense of humor, and a courageous protector of things that matter while holding loosely to those that don't. Encountering H—whether in the church, on the street, in city hall, or in the boardroom—left one permanently changed for the better. If one had to pick a word to summarize an encounter with H it would be the word good. Good in mind. Good in actions. Good in soul.

H, who contributed an essay to this volume, tragically passed away in the process of producing the book. In his goodness, he was in many ways an exemplar. H not only loved his hometown, Fresno, but cities around the world. His love for cities was formed and informed by a theological erudition encased in a streetwise moxie; an understanding of systems that was the bas-relief of actual people and, most importantly; a deep and abiding love for Jesus that saw, as St. Ignatius stated so well, "God in all things."

H now belongs to the communion of saints for all eternity where, among other things, we have complete confidence that he will continue to be the champion and cheerleader of the ideas and inspirations that this book, and his life, exemplify: seeing cities become God's playgrounds.

Acknowledgments

There is a riveting image in the book of Revelation. It occurs in the seventh chapter in verses 9–10 where the writer describes a "huge crowd, too huge to count" and that this crowd included everyone: "all nations, and tribes, all races and languages" singing praise to God.

While it would be a bit of an overstatement to say this Anthology represents a "crowd, too huge to count", it would not be altogether incorrect to say that it contains more than the usual suspects one might encounter in picking up a book. From the outset, it has been our firmest commitment and fiercest hope that this book could be compiled in such a way that a small hint of what Revelation describes could be glimpsed. That in these toxic times of tribalism a wide variety of reflections, touching on St. Paul's admonition in Galatians that there is no division in Christ, could be fashioned to tease into our minds eye a more concrete, compelling, and credible, sense of what the City As Playground can be. And, in the midst of its many varied dimensions and nuanced textures, it is our conviction that it indisputably starts and stops with an invitation to everyone. This Anthology and its 19 contributors are an exemplar of everyone.

It is in this spirit that we would like to acknowledge some individuals and institutions that made up the "huge crowd, too huge to count" thereby forming and informing this volume. We also want to bow in humble recognition to the futility of listing everyone. We trust that where we fail to mention your name or institution you will be given an interior consolation of grateful recognition.

To The Fetzer Institute, Mohammed Mohammed, and Chelsea Langston Bombino who saw the promise of this project and provided ongoing support and succor. This book would not have seen the light of day apart from their commitment. To Jack Fortin, who's theological acumen and organizational wisdom, have been vital in the work of LF, for writing the Foreword. To Daniel Cardinali whose wise counsel and indefatigable encouragement was ballast for the voyage. To BitterSweet Creative and in particular, Kate Schmidgall, Obiekwe Okolo, Dave Baker and Katie Hodge who achieved that greatest feat of alchemy and, as the poet Rumi states, "took our raggedness and made it silky".

To the 45+ conversation partners who became a part of the divine choreography that further confirmed our hunch of the appetite that exists for the idea of City As Playground. 19 of those have contributed their insights in these pages but we would be remiss not to mention the others that shared expertise and wisdom that informed the ideas contained in this collection. We are grateful to: Reid Carpenter, Founder of Leadership Foundations; Dr. Maria Fee, Artist, Theologian and Educator, Adjunct Assistant Professor of Theology and Culture at Fuller Theological Seminary; Cherie Harder, President of the Trinity Forum; Rev. Dr. David Odom, Executive director, Leadership Education at Duke Divinity School; Tod Bolsinger, Author and Senior Congregational Strategist and Associate

Professor of Leadership Formation at Fuller University; Chuck Mingo, Pastor and Co-Founder and CEO of LivingUNDIVIDED and WorkingUNDIVIDED; Peter Wehner, Senior Fellow at The Trinity Forum, contributing opinion writer for The New York Times, and a contributing editor for The Atlantic; Frederick Riley, Executive Director of Weave: The Social Fabric Project at The Aspen Institute; Eboo Patel, Founder and President of Interfaith America; Tom Locke, Former President of Texas Methodist Foundation; Blair Thompson-White, Director of Leadership Ministry for Texas Methodist Foundation; Lisa Greenwood, President of Texas Methodist Foundation; Jim Wallis, Author, Founder and Former Executive Director of Sojourners, Director of The Center on Faith and Justice at Georgetown University; Jim Simpson, Executive Director of the Center on Faith and Justice at Georgetown University; Rabbi Aaron Alexander, Rabbi of Adas Israel Congregation in Washington, DC; Mack McCarter, founder and coordinator of Community Renewal International; Mario Matos, Executive Director, Sinergia Leadership Foundation, Santo Domingo, Dominican Republic; Rev. Lina Thompson, Pastor Lake Burien Presbyterian Church; Rabbi Micah Greenstein, Rabbi of Temple Israel, Memphis, TN; Chris Lowney, author of Heroic Leadership: Best Practices from a 450-Year-Old Company That Changed the World; Father Patrick Kelly, SJ, PhD, Associate Professor, Religious Studies, University of Detroit Mercy; and; Devin Murphy, Partner, The Bridgespan Group.

G.K. Chesterton wrote, "But the reason we fly from the city is not in reality that it is not poetical; it is that its poetry is too fierce, too fascinating and too practical in its demands." It is with this quote in mind that a debt of gratitude is directed to the LF Global Board of Directors, the Global Network, and particularly, the Global Staff. At each turn, our colleagues supported us with enthusiasm, encouragement and thoughtful suggestions. With special thanks to Larry Lloyd, Kerri Feider, Melissa Monroe, Noah Baskett, Amy Nemeth, Christa Mooi, Rick Enloe, and Debbi Commodore who each contributed significantly to this project. Without LF's tireless commitment to not "fly from the city" but rather to see its "poetry" and say yes to the sharp edges of how "fierce", "fascinating" and "practical" cities and communities can be, this volume would be for naught. It is to these heroic women and men that we pray:

To God, be the glory;
To the earth, be peace;
To the people of good faith and goodwill, be courage;
And
To the cities and communities, be hope. Amen.

Dr. Dave Hillis and Jonathan Hayden

Table of Contents

viii

X

Foreword

Black Elk, the famed Oglala Lakota leader, said that "a vision without a task is just a dream. A task without a vision is drudgery. But a vision with a task can change the world." This quote captures the essence of this volume you have in your hands. I am convinced that these essays and interviews provide the bridge needed to join these two realities that are so critical to see cities around the world flourish.

The key to this bridge is metaphor. It is through our choice of metaphor that our imaginations and sense of wonder are unleashed, and we are released out of the swamp of drudgery. In short, vision and imagination are the fuel to make present what is not yet present. Whether it is seeing the city as a playground or another equally big idea, metaphors are essential in allowing us to see what could be and then, and only then, providing the necessary room for the tasks required to enact the vision.

The vision of seeing cities as playgrounds is what has always attracted me to Leadership Foundations (LF). It has what all great visions have: a modest beauty, elegant simplicity, and actionable steps only accessible by an empowered community. And the contributors to this anthology have done exactly that: they have placed before us a gigantic vision—what else is seeing the city as a playground if it is not that?—and they have given us the small steps to get there.

I should add, in full disclosure, that I have a particular personal interest in the Anthology and a hope and prayer that its message could spread deep and wide. Over the past number of years, I have had the privilege of being a member of the LF Global Board of Directors and Chair of LF's Colangelo Carpenter Innovation Center Trustee Council. My choice to serve in this way came as a result of many years of involvement on the Young Life staff and World Vision in executive roles, leading a thought leadership center at Luther Seminary where, as an ordained pastor in the Evangelical Lutheran Church of America (ELCA), I also was a Senior Lecturer. Currently I have the wonderful role and responsibility of serving at Augsburg University as a Senior Fellow. From this perch I can express without reservation the importance of this anthology and why I think it is an essential read for any individual and institution that is serious about the spiritual and social renewal of their respective city. Its essentialness rests on three ideas.

The first is the contributors understanding of the city as a living, breathing organism. Within each city sits specific organisms: city halls, school boards, businesses, nonprofits, and the like. Similar to the human body, the vision of cities as playgrounds protects it from any one organism being allowed to champion over another. It lifts up the idea that it is only in compilation and collaboration that we hear the wisdom of the city speak to its own needs thereby demanding a contextual approach. The genius of this volume is that it understands this critical truth which protects it from falling prey to becoming prescriptive which in turn is cancerous to the positive impact we all long to see.

The second idea each contributor understands is the difference between apprehension and comprehension. Comprehension is understanding by reason, to absorb something mentally. Apprehension is about taking hold of something. While comprehension is more reassuring, it is apprehension that allows us to live with the unknown. When these men and women write about a city, or play, or metaphors, they are participating in the holy act of apprehension. They speak with authority because they do not attempt to simply absorb a city as a mental and sociological construct. They have, because of their willingness to sit with the unknown and the uncomfortable, absorbed the city relationally and experientially. They have apprehended it.

The third idea is that this anthology is birthed out of reflective experience. It has cut its teeth on things that matter and impact people's lives. The contributors are people who I have either known by friendship and/or reputation and have passed that severest of tests when we consider positive change in the public square: poetically articulating a theory of possibility while prosaically laying out concrete practices. They have gained their wisdom through the practice of action and reflection. Because of this, they are perfectly positioned to guide us through this big idea. The essays and interviews provide slivers of theological and practical ways of seeing the city as a playground.

While LF figures prominently in this anthology, it is not a book about them. Rather, it is a book that invites us all to consider how we might work in unison. We really are better together.

The beauty of an anthology is that we don't have to read everything all at once. It can be approached from multiple fronts. As an example, here is a strange habit of mine: I read books backwards, even novels. I like to know where the author arrived so that I can retrace how they got there. So, with this anthology, as a lifelong practitioner of loving cities, I favor reading the works that show the outcomes the authors achieved in wrestling with this gigantic vision. How did the vision play out in real time? Once this is clear I then go back and read the theological and philosophical reflections that sit at the foundations of these practices. I suspect that some will do the opposite of me where they prefer to have an understanding of the philosophical and then read how it shows up in practice. Regardless, I would like to give you permission to read this anthology according to your own learning style, while keeping in mind that we absolutely need both the vision and the tasks that Black Elk articulated. Only then can the world be changed, and our cities become what they were intended to be in the first place: playgrounds.

Rev. Dr. Jack Fortin

Senior Fellow, Augsburg University and Board Chair, Leadership Foundations

〰〰〰〰〰〰〰〰〰〰〰〰〰〰〰〰〰

🏐 🏀 🎾 ⚽

If you want to change the world, change your metaphor.

—Joseph Campbell

⚐ ⊕ ◯ ⚽

Metaphors have a way of holding
the most truth in the least space.

—Orson Scott Card

xvi

Preface

The purpose of this anthology is to delve more deeply into this idea of Campbell's and the ramifications of what a metaphor change might entail as it relates to the work of the social and spiritual renewal of cities and communities.

Fundamentally, metaphor is a way of seeing. It is a figure of speech in which a term or phrase is used to depict or suggest a resemblance. The power of a metaphor is that it directs our line of sight and therefore guides our behavior and interactions. Stanley Hauerwas, a noted theologian from Duke Divinity, hinted at the gravitas of Campbell's statement when he wrote, "We can only act within the world in which we see." We believe this to be true—we can only act within the world we can see—and any path forward and its corresponding clarity will largely be the result of the metaphors we choose. George Lakoff and Mark Johnson go even further in their groundbreaking book, *Metaphors We Live By:* "Metaphor is for most people a device of the poetic imagination and the rhetorical flourish—a matter of extraordinary rather than ordinary language. Moreover, metaphor is typically viewed as characteristic of language alone, a matter of words rather than thought or action. For this reason, most people think they can get along perfectly well without metaphor. We have found, on the contrary, that metaphor is pervasive in everyday life, not just in language but in thought and action. Our ordinary conceptual system, in terms of which we both think and act, is fundamentally metaphorical in nature." [i]

So, it falls on us to do the very important work of cultivating and curating the metaphors by which and through which we see, interpret, and act in the world and our cities.

Metaphors are not only useful rhetorically, but scientific studies have also proven that they physically affect the way we perceive the world. They can change the way our brains interpret an issue and how we respond to it. In one study by Paul H. Thibodeau and Lera Boroditsky, participants were asked to respond to a story about crime in their cities, framed by two different metaphors. In one, crime was described as a "beast," "lurking" and "preying." In the other, crime was a "virus" that was "infecting" the city. While the rest of the facts in the story were the same, those who now saw crime as a "beast" wanted criminals imprisoned with harsh punishments. When presented with the idea that crimes were a "virus," participants wanted social reform that would address the root causes.

Said another way, the idea of seeing the city as a playground rather than a battleground is more than just a poetic means to help us frame collaborative action in a city or community, but it can actually change the way we see and act collectively.

The Jesuit poet Gerard Manley Hopkins hints at how this process of choosing metaphors can begin when he penned the following: "Acts in God's eye what in God's eye he is—Christ—for Christ plays in ten thousand places, lovely in limbs, and lovely in eyes not his." Hopkins touches on the importance of this process of how seeing turns into acting by providing a theological nudge ("what in God's eye he is") and an anthropological whisper (God sees in us "Christ" who already "plays in ten thousand places"). Anaïs Nin heightens what is at stake in our choice of metaphor by stating: "We don't see things as they are; we see them as we are." However, it is Jesus (as is often the case) that provides the bridge between Hopkins' more aspirational tone and Nin's more somber sense of the importance of how we see is developed when he states: "The eye is the lamp of the body. If your eyes are good, your whole body will be full of light" (Matthew 6:22). For Jesus, the implication is clear: how we see is directly correlated to the degree to which light exists in us, which in turn, will determine how we act. Important is the agency implicit in Jesus' statement: will we choose to have eyes that are good? Our argument is that whether or not we have "good eyes" has everything to do with the metaphor(s) we choose, as that determines how we see this world. We believe that the metaphor that is most needed to engage the spiritual and social renewal of cities and communities, to see through the eyes of Christ, is to see them as God's playgrounds rather than battlegrounds

What hangs in the balance is none other than the agency needed to make positive change. Through the metaphor of a playground, we begin to chisel away at the artifice and machinations of the battleground. A currency of relationships replaces a culture of transaction. A spirit of inclusion displaces a need for exclusion. A love of a particular geography for the sake of its own end erases the noxious notion of place as an opportunity for extraction. And religion refuses to be instrumentalized and becomes the gracious elixir of the common good. Our further argument is that much of the partisan bickering, pyrotechnic tribalism, and histrionic contortions is due less to rational disagreements and more to the unexamined and unexplored metaphors by which we see and act in relationship to one another which causes untold damage.

Two quick notes that will be picked up in further detail in the ensuing chapters. The first is what we mean by "play." What we don't mean is a kind of frivolous, nonserious, and impractical approach to cities. Rather, we believe that the posture of play produces a seriousness of purpose and simultaneously allows us to take ourselves less seriously, which we believe is a needed antidote for our troubled times. The second is the reality that a playground as a metaphor is vulnerable to the criticism of being a bit pollyannaish and even preposterous; that it softens or neglects the harsh realities that are present in all our cities. This will be dealt with in the later essays, but we do want to make this simple observation:

xxi

The power of this metaphor is precisely because it does take into account that playgrounds have bullies.

It is only as we acknowledge the reality of a bully that we can begin to see why and how we need to join forces to prevent them from making our playgrounds into battlegrounds.

Through this anthology, we will attempt to take the metaphor of seeing the city as a playground and explore its implications from different angles, perspectives, and ever fresh applications. We have asked several thought leaders and practitioners in different disciplines and domains to describe how their thinking and work might be impacted through the use of this metaphor.

The 19 reflections in this anthology represent 40+ interviews, each designed to drill down into how the metaphor might impact the contributors' respective work, positively and negatively. We also looked to explore where any flat sides or obstacles might exist in the course of operationalizing this metaphor.

Drs. David Hillis, Dale Irvin, Luke Bretherton, Terry McGonigal and Father James Alison provide theological and philosophical reflections on the intellectual weight and import of city as playground. Their work covers the waterfront from stories of origin, church history, the biblical idea of shalom, and what this all means for one's ecclesiological and anthropological proclivities. Kerry Alys Robinson, Curtis Chang, Romanita Hairston, Dr. H. Spees, Chelsea Langston Bombino and Dr. Troy Jackson are what we call table-setters. This group also includes transcribed conversations with Rev. Jen Bailey, Father James Martin, Aaron Dorfman and Dr.

Mark Labberton. Each contributor offers thoughtful reflections on what specific issues of engagement surface as one sees their city as a playground. These range from the function of language itself, the nature of institutions, spiritual formation, falling in love with a city and racial reconciliation. These are real time views of how we grapple with the idea both in theory and in praxis. Finally, but by no means lastly, we have a group of practitioners who are taking all of these ideas and concepts and working them out. These include Abhishek Gier in Delhi, Dr. Randy White in Fresno, Rev. Noel Castellanos in Central America and Blinky Rodriguez in Los Angeles. All ask the very specific questions of how the idea of seeing one's city as a playground makes a practical difference and, if it does, what do these differences look like?

To help you access this Anthology, we have created four sections that weave together the three strands mentioned above: the academic, table setters and practitioners. It is our hope that this mix will be the right dosage that will allow you to simultaneously engage your head, heart and hands.

Leadership Foundations and The Fetzer Institute decided to engage in this project together because of two shared interests. The first is a deep belief that any meaningful change for the better in this world must involve spiritual engagement—a spirituality characterized by inclusion rather than exclusion, engagement rather than rivalry, and a playful yet sober purposefulness. The second is a conviction that the ultimate healing agent required is to reestablish the simple truth of loving relationships—that our relational nature precedes our rationalism and tending to this becomes the animating force for all we are and hope to do.

Over the past 40+ years, anchored by this central metaphor and guiding vision, the Leadership Foundations global network has sat with the question of what it would look like to operationalize City As Playground in cities and communities around the world. What, for example, might take place as we consider the City As Playground in places like Delhi and Dallas, Pretoria and Pittsburgh, Santo Domingo and Savannah? How would programs and initiatives look different? In what ways would interfaith and nonfaith dialogue be impacted? How would staff of different organizations working on similar issues see each other and the cities they serve? What has been achieved to date has been astounding and begs to be explored in ever greater and deeper ways.

Enter The Fetzer Institute (TFI). Fetzer, who exists to help build the spiritual foundation for a loving world, has given its considerable skill to create a remarkable set of resources and supports for those doing this kind of work. Fetzer, "believes in the possibility of a loving world: a world where TFI and partners understand we are all part of one human family and know our lives have purpose. In the world we seek, everyone is committed to courageous compassion and bold love—powerful forces for good in the face of fear, anger, division, and despair."

The hoped for and anticipated outcomes of this anthology are threefold: 1) a curated resource of thoughtful reflections would be available for leaders throughout the world who are committed to the spiritual and social renewal of their respective cities; 2) that a platform will be built to facilitate ongoing conversations between practitioners and theorists and; 3) the leadership of those who access these reflections and this platform would find that their competency and capacity were demonstrably increased.

In the film *Gladiator*, one particular line of dialogue captures the essence of this anthology. The line is spoken early in the picture, soon after the victory of the storied military commander Maximus Decimus Meridius in Germania and shortly before Emperor Marcus Aurelius' death. Aware of his son's incapacity to succeed him as leader, the emperor asks Maximus to take his place as lord protector of Rome. Maximus balks at the request, whereby the two begin a discussion of the city itself: what it was, what it had become, and what it could be. Marcus Aurelius, aware that without some decisive action Rome would not make it through the winter, expresses his thoughts to Maximus: "There was once a dream that was Rome. You could only whisper it. Anything more than a whisper and it would vanish; it was so fragile." It is our hope and prayer that this anthology will help you think about your city and community, fragile as it might be, with a new hope that you can, once again, begin to whisper.

i Metaphors We Live By; *George Lakoff and Mark Johnson; University of Chicago Press; 1980; pg. 3*

ONE.

CITY
As
PLAYGROUND

Dr. Dave Hillis

Leadership Foundations

For thousands of years cities have been the gathering places where human beings have sought protection, been exploited, taken chances, brought innovations, and met despair. Nowhere else on Earth has hope and death, love and spite, promise and catastrophe more closely comingled than in cities. We've run toward, escaped from, navigated through, circumvented, and hidden ourselves within the human city—for good and for ill. But while humans are inclined toward isolation—creating artifices of grandiosity and self, constantly building our little kingdoms of certitude and separation—we are also drawn inexorably toward one another. As Jane Jacobs noted many years ago, "There is no logic that can be superimposed on the city; people make it, and it is to them, not buildings, that we must fit our plans."

Cities promise much and routinely disappoint and we should not be surprised that humanity has always been trying to understand what a city is, why we seek it or avoid it, how to treat it, what it's for. Questions loom: Is the city an accident or a necessary evil? Is it a useful means to a preferred end? Should we seize it, conquer it, grit our teeth and bear it? Escape it for a faraway post in the countryside, exchanging the din of car alarms for the companionable chirping of crickets? All of these options depend on which metaphor you choose to see the city through. As noted in the Preface, Stanley Hauerwas, American theologian and professor of theological ethics at Duke Divinity School, writes in Resident Aliens: "We can only act within the world in which we see. Vision is the necessary prerequisite for ethics." And since vision is a result of metaphors, then the most critical decision we make is the metaphor we select and embody.

Behold: An Encounter

If there is a singular word that sits at the heart of the founding of Leadership Foundations' (LF) story and the idea of the city as playground rather than a battleground it is the word behold. Behold is the bigger and more muscular cousin to a number of family members: look, see, contemplate, discern, regard, perceive and distinguish to name a few. But it is bigger and broader because to behold is to take in not only one's perceptions of something or someone, but to recognize the element of encounter. To behold is to encounter something that is happening in the present tense, not something that happened previously, or you hope to have happen in the future. It is to engage a new reality that is currently happening; to receive a new way of seeing that will not leave you the same. It is Moses at the burning bush; Isaiah before the heavenly throne; Paul on the road to Damascus. Shakespeare may have had this idea of encounter in mind when he expressed the following in *A Midsummer Night's Dream.* He says: "The poet's eye, in a fine frenzy rolling, doth glance from heaven to Earth, from Earth to heaven; And as imagination bodies forth the forms of things unknown, the poet's pen turns them to shapes, and gives to airy nothing a local habitation and a name." To behold, nestled within the "glance from heaven to Earth, from Earth to heaven" ...and acting as "imagination bodies forth the forms of things unknown" has long been the tradition of poets, prophets, and practitioners. Women and men engaged, or more precisely, being engaged by something that stood outside them while simultaneously penetrating the present reality.

Pittsburgh, Sam Shoemaker, and Reid Carpenter

For LF, the initial moment of *behold* occurred when the Rev. Dr. Samuel Shoemaker took Reid Carpenter to Mt. Washington in 1962. As they stood on Mount Washington overlooking the city of Pittsburgh, Sam asked Reid to behold the city of Pittsburgh. Reid describes his experience of beholding Pittsburgh with Sam and Don James as follows:

One day in 1962, as he had done countless times before, Sam took me and a few men up to the top of Mount Washington. He guided us onto the overlook in front of St. Mary's on the Mount, giving us a breathtaking view of the river-ways and across the muscle-bound city of steel. And Sam commanded us to "behold, our city." And we beheld. We beheld the belching smoke of the steel mills lining the muddy riverbank down the Monongahela River to our right. We beheld the heavily laden barges maneuvering small mountains of coal westward into the broad Ohio River to our left. We beheld the crisscrossing of the rivers by its many bridges. Straight ahead, we beheld the movement of trucks and buses and cars and pedestrians racing to keep to their schedules, hustling back and forth to appointments across the city. And we beheld the great buildings that stood just before them in Pittsburgh's Golden Triangle, the glass and steel and aluminum rising up to frame the city's skyline, doing justice to its standing at that time as America's third largest corporate center.

Reid, who was then just twenty-four years old and the Pittsburgh-area director of Young Life, further recounts his experience atop Mount Washington:

As I beheld my newly adopted city it was though a spark settled in the dry tinder of my heart and I beheld what Pittsburgh could become, what God intended for this great city.

As Reid continues to tell this story, standing on the very same spot many years later, he falls silent as he again looks out over the city, remembering that day with Sam, and how, for the very first time, his own eyes saw the vast network of connections and relationships that make up the complex organism that is a city.

I recognized how people who owned the companies, people who made the city run day to day, people who worked in the mills and on those barges, and the kids we worked with in Young Life, were all connected. It suddenly felt like things had a capacity to be manageable in Pittsburgh...and then Sam said these remarkable words as we beheld our city: 'I have a vision that one day Pittsburgh will become as famous for God as it now is for steel.'

The passion in Reid's voice still captures what happened inside him that day.

And it was like it was a voice from God, he added, *announcing that God had a special intention for the city of Pittsburgh and maybe for cities all over the world if only we could behold them!*

What happens inside the kind of city that shows God off? How do the people behave in such a city? What do their businesses do? The hospitals and schools? And most importantly, what becomes of the poor? Although a city can often be ugly, harsh, and sharp-edged, even the most superficial first look at the city will tell us that it has an endless number of stories of the human image to unfold. What was needed was an image, a shape, a container, a vehicle that could carry Sam's vision forward.

What became clear to Reid at that moment was what the Holy Spirit was up to in Pittsburgh: She was playing. And our task was to align ourselves with what she was already doing. Playing, not in a frivolous, facile, or fluky kind of way, but rather a playfulness that was focused, innovative, and eternally creative. In short, what God was doing was moving Pittsburgh and, perhaps all cities, toward becoming more like playgrounds instead of battlegrounds.

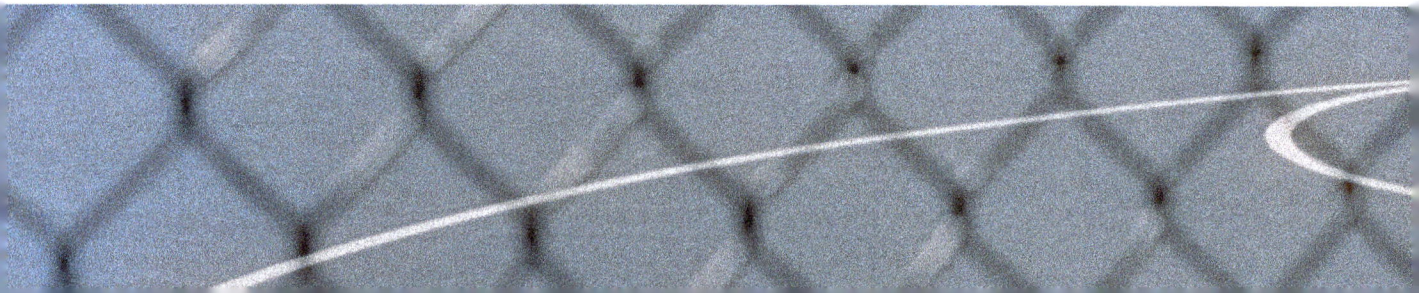

God's Love Affair With Cities

Of course the idea of seeing the city as a playground did not start with Sam and Reid. God's love affair with cities has a number of threads that, when woven together, become a tapestry of affection, pathos and beauty for cities that are unrivaled in other sacred scriptures. Beginning with the first city in the Bible, Enoch, that becomes a surrogate protector for its first mayor Cain, to cities of refugee in the book of Numbers, to Jonah's complicated relationship with the city of Nineveh, to Jesus weeping over the city of Jerusalem, to St. Paul's urban strategy in Acts, to the book of Revelation's vision of the heavenly Jerusalem becoming our final destination — all pulse with the energy and desire of a God who understands the gift of cities, what they can be, and how we should dwell in them. The clearest expression of the city as God's playground occurs in the book of Zechariah. Jerusalem had fallen on hard times and was anything but a playground. The book of Zechariah was written to assist in the rebuilding of the Temple, which had been destroyed by the Babylonians who put them into exile. In the eighth chapter, Zechariah has the audacity to declare the following to the inhabitants of Jerusalem: "Old men and old women will come back to Jerusalem, sit on benches on the streets and spin tales, move around safely with their canes — a good city to grow old in. And boys and girls will fill the public parks, laughing and playing — a good city to grow up in" (Zechariah 8:4 – 5; The Message). It was a good city to grow up in because, presciently, Zechariah understood that the two most vulnerable people groups of any city are the very old and the very young. It goes without saying that if those two groups are doing well it means the city herself is functioning as she should. In Zechariah's vision, the city has literally become a playground.

The idea of seeing the city as God's playground rather than a battleground changes our perspective in three important ways. They are the "necessary prerequisites for ethics", noted by Hauerwas, if a positive change is going to be made in the social and spiritual renewal of cities.

The first is theological. Cities, Lewis Mumford argues, have always had a spiritual foundation. God is decidedly a friend of the city rather than a foe. Cities are God's idea. God delights in her smells, tastes, shape, and people. Understanding this gives us confidence that God is deeply committed to her flourishing. That God is working alongside us rather than against us. That ultimately, since cities are God's idea, that while the Bible starts with the story of humankind in a garden its final consumption is in a city.

The second is sociological. Martin Luther King Jr. famously stated, "In a real sense all life is interrelated. All men are caught in an inescapable network of mutuality, tied in a single garment of destiny. Whatever affects one directly, affects all indirectly." Seeing the city as a playground allows us to see that our fellow citizens are colleagues rather than competitors. They are assets rather than deficits. We can distance ourselves from the contentious world of petty rivalry and cultivate a world of generosity where all win.

The third is economic. Walter Brueggemann has written widely that the fundamental through-line in the Old Testament is the battle between the scarcity mindset of Pharoah and abundance mindset of the God of Israel. By seeing the city as a playground, we see a world of abundance rather than scarcity and that resources are accessible to all. Money, ideas, practices, and time are considered properties to be shared because there is enough for everyone. When we see the economy this way, we find ourselves more in the habit of giving than taking.

5

The Future

As we consider the idea of the future, whatever else it might be, we know it will be an urban reality. 56 percent of the world's population currently lives in urban areas and 66 percent are expected to live in cities by 2050. Which norms and institutions we create to support this reality will be a choice that will ripple outward to shape social and organizational assumptions far beyond a dense downtown.

As a result, the importance of the way we see our cities cannot be overstated. It will dictate how we approach them, whether we live in them, how we interface with the individuals and institutions that fill them. This will be true for all of us whether we are people of good faith or good will, but there is a particular aspect of seeing the city as God's playground that Christians need to engage. Father William Lynch S.J. writes,

> *The city of man/woman may very well not be Christian; but it cannot do without Christians. It is a life and a community under God which all men/women of good will must work to save — a community of charity for citizens where all men/women can live in a unity whether of scholarship or of economy or of peace. For a Christian to create catacombs rather than to enter into the city would be a terrible mistake.*

What is to prevent Christians from creating "catacombs" rather than to "enter into the city?"

It will depend, in the same way it occurred for Reid with Sam, on what we behold. Will we reach for a metaphor that insulates, protects, and further divides or one that inspires, prospers, and unites? Denise Levertov, as she often does, beautifully articulates the choice:

> *The killings continue, each second*
> *pain and misfortune extend themselves*
> *in the genetic chain, injustice is done knowingly,*
>   *and the air*
> *bears the dust of decayed hopes,*
> *yet breathing those fumes, walking the thronged*
> *pavements among crippled lives, jackhammers*
> *raging, a parking lot painfully agleam*
> *in the May sun, I have seen*
> *not behind but within, within the*
> *dull grief, blown grit, hideous*
> *concrete facades, another grief, a gleam*
> *as of dew, an abode of mercy,*
> *have heard not behind but within noise*
> *a humming that drifted into a quiet smile.*
> *Nothing was changed, all was revealed otherwise;*
> *not that horror was not, not that killings did not*
>   *continue,*
> *but that as if transparent all disclosed*
> *an otherness that was blessed, that was bliss.*
> *I saw Paradise in the dust of the street.*

Cities will in fact become better if people like us courageously choose to see and love them with the wit, will, and wisdom that Levertov raises up: Cities As Playgrounds.

BELIEF, IMAGINATION, CREATIVITY, JOY

Building Blocks of Urban Renewal

Kerry Alys Robinson

Founding Executive Director of Leadership Roundtable
and current Executive Director of the Opus Prize Foundation

Some things must be believed to be seen. Just ask anyone who has brought to fruition a seemingly impossible goal.

Visionaries are believers with intoxicating passion, even while they are dismissed as quixotic at best or irrational at worst. True visionaries are tenacious, compelling, animated and exactingly descriptive. And the language visionaries employ — and this cannot be overstated — matters. Words and choice of words fuel their power of persuasion. It defines the potential at hand.

For eleven years, as the founding executive director of Leadership Roundtable, I had a standing weekly meeting with our founding chairman of the board, Geoff Boisi, a testament of our commitment to accountability, mission, and mutual respect. It provided the opportunity to report on progress, flag challenges, and strategize for the future. When I look back, meeting with Geoff on a weekly basis was among one of the greatest privileges of my life. To have the investment of such an accomplished, intuitive, dedicated, and generous ally was and has been lifechanging. However, I didn't think of it that way in the beginning. Early on in my time with Geoff I found myself referring to our weekly call as "my day of reckoning." Over time, the emotional effect of a silly use of a serious phrase was anxiety-provoking. It was diminishing my time with Geoff by creating an anxiety-laced and emotionally charged time that was stealing the opportunity for awe of being with such a remarkable man. Words matter, even when we are not conscious of the effect of the words we employ. Reflecting on it, I wondered why I would characterize the weekly meeting this way, even glibly, when the very opposite was true. I immediately altered the phrase from "day of reckoning" to "day of recognition" creating the conditions for joyful anticipation rather than dread, celebration rather than regret. That change made a measurable difference in productivity, positive emotional resonance, creativity, and gratitude.

And this lesson has carried over. I have spent my entire adult life working in the philanthropic and faith-based nonprofit sector. Core to the flourishing of these sectors is fundraising. And yet, consider the words we resort to when casually discussing the activity of raising money. "Hit her up for money." "Put the squeeze on him." "Target them." This is the language of violation, not invitation. The vernacular of scarcity rather than abundance. Is it any wonder that so many leaders in the nonprofit sector bring cognitive dissonance to the important, life-giving work of raising money? My intuition is that the dissonance is largely due to how we choose to acquire and assemble language.

I had been considering the importance of language for years when I had the immense good fortune to meet Dave Hillis, Leadership Foundations' long-time president and now senior innovation fellow at the Colangelo Carpenter Innovation Center. With impeccable clarity and characteristic humility, he described his work in a single sentence: "What if we saw our cities as God's playgrounds rather than as battlegrounds?" My imagination leapt with the unlimited potential of what our cities as God's playgrounds could—must, will—look like. A playground and a battleground are diametrically opposite. And it all came down to whether you choose to place "play" or "battle" in front of "ground."

Choosing the word playground immediately conjured up memories of taking my children to parks in fresh air to play with all the attendant images and associations. Playgrounds are about laughter, creativity, energy, joy, childlike inhibition, color, friendship, sunshine, timelessness, and imagination. As an adult and a parent, playgrounds provided a chance to be present to what matters most. There is freedom on a playground, to be sure, but there are also rules of engagement: share, take turns, no bullying, be kind, apologize, include. Be care-full. Look out for the little ones. The playground belongs to everyone.

By choosing the word playground we are declaring that we live in a place of social engagement. And social engagement leads to community, the antidote to isolation and loneliness. Community and belonging, discovering what we have and cherish in common through our commitment to diversity becomes a corrective to fear and the advent of renewal. Seeing a city as a playground moves us to understand our cities as places of assets rather than deficits.

Cities are home to more than half of the world's population, and that is expected to increase in the decades to come. We must get this right, right now. There is an urgency to the invitation to see differently.

Persisting in a framework that posits cities as battlegrounds means many will be afraid to engage and believe they lack the expertise or capability to contribute to positive solutions. They will quite literally simply aim to survive, largely by disengagement or self-protection.

Instead of a problem to be solved, a battle to be won, we have an opportunity to exercise creativity and imagination. Serious skills are needed in this context. People who design and manage playgrounds and ensure their safety are serious people, highly trained, weighing many considerations. Innovation in design, safety, and engineering is utilized to make playgrounds safer and more accessible, ever more intriguing and inviting. It will be through our language that we see these assets in ever more profound and generous ways.

Reframing the way we see cities as God's playground, rather than as a human battleground, also invites the faith dimension, rooted in shared values, to be an integral part of urban design and policy implementation. Faith at its most authentic is an invitation to full participation, rather than a posture of defensiveness. And what God and playgrounds have in common is joy. Pierre Teilhard de Chardin said it best, "Joy is the infallible sign of the presence of God."

If we choose to implement and employ the right language, we will see our assets in ever more profound and generous ways. We are not creating cities from scratch. There are assets at our disposal. What seeing the city as a playground invites us into is an important and irresistible point of departure. Children are the primary beneficiaries of our playgrounds which is an especially helpful paradigm for the work we do today to renew our cities. This is a framework that allows for everyone to been seen as a creature of God and that they be given the benefits of human dignity and the responsibilities of caring for the common good.

There are some promising examples of cities as playgrounds. Mack McCarter, the founder and coordinator of Community Renewal International (CRI) and 2022 Opus Prize laureate, is committed to changing the world block by block, neighborhood by neighborhood, city by city. For Mack, God is at the center of the equation, hard wiring us to love and to care for one another in the first place. CRI's methodology is predicated on the belief that the vast

Some things must be

majority of humankind cares. That we care is what we have in common and if we can be conscious of it, we can create intentionally caring and nurturing communities. Applying the Catholic principle of subsidiarity, the idea is that local communities know best how to strengthen their communities. Where CRI is present, crime has fallen by 60 percent. As Mack says, "Caring alone won't save the world, but caring together will."

We also have the examples of cities which have prioritized the arts, which is reflected in their budgets, secured by public policy, and evidenced by public exhibition. Art is simply good for the soul, a measure of health, and an important investment in the future. Children who create will not destroy.

Another asset at our disposal is what we can learn from the past. One of the critiques of urban renewal and other mid-20th century urban planning decisions was the displacement and further segregation of people. We have the opportunity to envision 21st century cities that undo policies that made them siloed and exclusive, and instead become places of inclusivity where everyone of all ages, races, incomes, ethnicities, and vocations properly understand that the city belongs to them. This playground, this city, is for everyone. Similarly, a strategy for the renewal of our cities in the 21st century must prioritize the safety of the city itself, for example by prioritizing green infrastructure, access to green space, climate resilience for coastal cities, and pedestrian safety.

To achieve this, I go back to where I started: Some things must be believed to be seen. In order to be seen, they need to be described. And to be described, we need each other. Whether it is the visionary, poet, artist, advocate, urban planner, architect, environmentalist, engineer, community organizer, policy maker, gardener, or parent, all have the power to describe our possible reality. All people who care are needed. We can do this.

believed to be seen.

THE LITURGY OF THE WORLD

Dr. Dale T. Irvin

Founding faculty member of the New School of Biblical Theology
and Former President of New York Theological Seminary

John Chrysostom was one of the most important figures in the Christian movement in the fourth and early fifth centuries. His influence upon the churches of the world continues today. *Chrysostom* in Greek means *golden-tongued* or *golden-mouthed.*

It was not just his rhetorical eloquence that earned him his reputation as a preacher, however. In 398 Chrysostom was appointed by the emperor as archbishop of Constantinople. Established as the capital of the Roman Empire only six decades earlier, Constantinople had quickly become one of the wealthiest cities in the world at the time. Constantinople was a city of severe inequalities. As the Archbishop in the city, Chrysostom did not hesitate to point them out. He regularly denounced such inequalities in no uncertain terms in the cathedral to the imperial household and others who were part of the upper class. The wealth that we control does not belong to us, he constantly reminded his listeners. We are stewards of whatever wealth we have. God is the owner and requires us to manage these resources for the good of all people. In a sermon on the parable of Lazarus and the rich man, for instance, he said:

> *I beg that, chiefest of all, you will remember constantly that not to share your own riches with the poor is robbery of the poor, and a depriving them of their livelihood; and that what we possess is not only our own, but also theirs.* [i]

His prophetic stance on such matters did not go unnoticed. A synod was called in 403 in Constantinople with bishops from other regions, including the patriarch of Alexandria, to consider a number of theological charges of heresy that were made against Chrysostom. The main charge leveled against him was his supposed support for the teachings of Origen of Alexandria, who had died 150 years earlier. Underlying these charges was the resistance to his public pronouncements condemning the inequalities of wealth and poverty in the city. Chrysostom was found guilty and deposed.

made from stone like the stone that was rolled away from the tomb of Christ. This was the altar upon which the eucharist continued to be celebrated. But the hearts of those who communed there would remain stone as well if they were not brought to the third altar, which was found not inside the church, but outside in the wider city. This was the altar of the poor, the beggars, and others who were downcast in the city, he explained:

> This altar mayest thou everywhere see lying, both in lanes and in marketplaces, and mayest sacrifice upon it every hour; for on this too is sacrifice performed. And as the priest stands invoking the Spirit, so dost thou too invoke the Spirit, not by speech, but by deeds. [iv]

Serving the poor was not just comparable to celebrating the eucharist; it completed it. Drawing on the work of Chrysostom, Ion Bria calls the work of justice in the world the "liturgy after the liturgy" in Christian life. [v]

Liturgy and Playgrounds

The notion that addressing inequalities of wealth in the city is a Christian liturgical rite might seem at first to be at odds with the long tradition of Christian practices. In their recent study of the various liturgical rites of the seven major traditions of Eastern Orthodox Christianity (identified as "Armenian, Byzantine, Coptic, Ethiopian, East Syrian, West Syrian, and Maronite"), Maxwell E. Johnson and Stefanos Alexopoulos make no reference to Chrysostom's notion of the liturgy on the altar of the poor. [vi] There is not even a passing reference to Bria's book, which seeks to address directly the intrinsic connection between worship and work in the world.

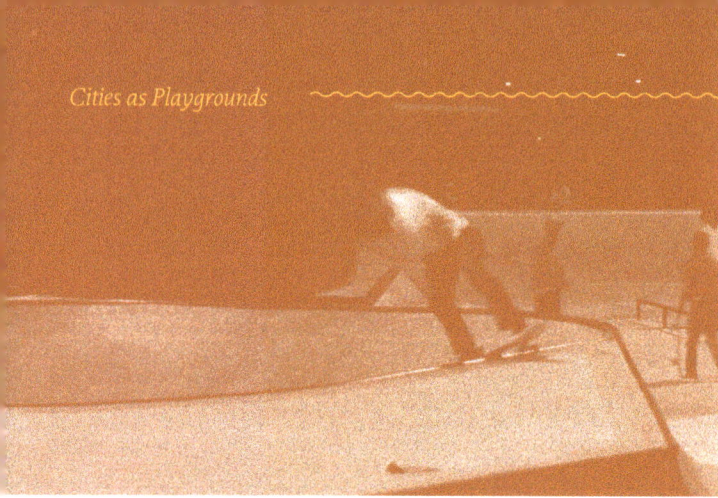

Chrysostom and Liturgy

Chrysostom's legacy in Christian history does not rest only on the prophetic stance he took regarding the poor. He also had a major impact on the liturgical life of churches throughout the world. Among his major accomplishments was the arrangement of the main order of worship, known in Eastern Orthodoxy as the Divine Liturgy. To this day, Eastern Orthodox churches throughout the world continue to follow *The Divine Liturgy of Saint John Chrysostom* in their services of worship each Sunday. [ii] Chrysostom did not compose the liturgy from scratch. Most of the content of the liturgy including the prayers and praises offered is drawn directly from biblical passages. As with almost all ancient Christian liturgies, worship included the reading of generous portions of scripture followed by a homily or sermon, and the celebration of the eucharist with bread and wine. In the case of *The Divine Liturgy of Saint John Chrysostom*, his name is closely identified with the most sacred part of the liturgy, the anaphora, or what in the Western Latin tradition is usually called the eucharistic prayer, in which the bread and wine are consecrated to become the body and blood of Christ.

For most Christians, liturgy is something that takes place entirely within a church building. This was not so for Chrysostom. In a remarkable sermon delivered most likely when he was serving as a priest in Antioch before becoming archbishop of Constantinople, [iii] Chrysostom said that there were three altars in Christian life. The first was the altar of the cross itself on which Christ had offered himself as a sacrifice. This altar was in turn encountered through two other altars at which we continue to meet the Risen Christ, he said. The second was the altar in the sanctuary of the church,

The Handbook for Liturgical Studies traces the etymological origins of the word liturgy to the ancient Greek word, *leitourgia*. *Leitourgia* in turn was derived from a combination of two other Greek words, *laos* (translated into English as "people") and *ergon* (translated as "work"). *Leitourgia,* according to Anscar J. Chupungo, OSB, originally meant *public works* or state projects in Greek. [vii] Naphtali Lewis goes further to explain that the term in Greek originally referred to "specific state services required of wealthy citizens and residents." [viii] Often it entailed expenditure of funds for public works or celebrations and other events. Eventually it also entailed services provided by the wealthy from enslaved persons under their control.

Reducing the meaning of "liturgy" to its manifestation in acts of worship that take place within a church sanctuary prevents us from being able to see the liturgical work taking place out in the wider city. Liturgy is a form of ritual. [ix] Like all ritual acts, the meaning is found in its actual performance, without being reducible to the empirical dimensions. Seeing the *more*, the surplus of meaning that is located in common human experiences entails an act of interpretation, which in turn flows from what David Tracy classically termed the "analogical imagination." [x]

Tracy draws his theological argument for the centrality of the analogical imagination from Thomas Aquinas. [xi] Indeed, the entire system of theology that Thomas built is guided by the principle that analogies and the broader process of analogical thinking provide positive knowledge regarding God, who is always more than our understanding. I will not try here to unpack to any significant extent the centrality of Thomas' analogical method. Others

have done that much better than I ever could. I would simply note here, however, that for Thomas, closely related to the intellectual realm of analogical thinking is that of metaphorical thinking.

Thomas did not collapse all analogical thinking into metaphorical thinking, but he recognized the two were closely related. Saying, "God is good," is analogical in that it depends upon us already having a notion of goodness that is then extended to God without being exhaustive. The divine goodness extends far beyond any experience of human goodness but is continuous with it enough to make for a meaningful statement. Saying, "God is a rock," on the other hand, is a metaphor. It asserts the similarity of the divine with a limited, sensible object. Metaphors are less abstract than other forms of analogical thinking. Furthermore, argues Robert Masson, metaphors have a more disruptive effect than other forms of analogical thinking. [xii] They introduce an element into the analogical process that would not usually be otherwise expected.

Sally McFague picks up on this more disruptive process of thinking and talking about God. She grounds the entire theological project of thinking and talking about God in the parabolic teachings of Jesus. [xiii] All theology, she argues, is or ought to be metaphorical in its efforts and outcomes. [xiv] Metaphors move us more rapidly from one place to another in our thinking. Mary Zournazi makes the point well: "In Greece, the vehicles of mass transportation are called *messa metaphorai.* To go to work in Greece, or to come home, one can take a metaphor—a bus or a train." [xv]

15

Locating metaphors, and by extension metaphorical theology, in the streets of the city is important for us as we look for those third altars in the life of our wider urban environments. I suggest here that the liturgy that takes place on those altars that Chrysostom identified with the life of the poor is not only that of sacrifice. The city is a place filled with rituals, from the morning commute on the busses and trains, the *messa metaphorai*, to the endless evenings of dining and banqueting. Some of these rituals are small and pass mostly unnoticed, like the ceremonial greeting of a handshake or a bow, or the morning cup of tea or coffee. Others amount to greater levels of meaning and remembrance. The gala banquets associated with fundraising, for instance, but also the rituals of office life and government processes are part of the overall urban environment. Parades are one form of grand urban rituals with which we are quite familiar. The theater is another. Sporting events where children and adults alike are at play are yet a third.

This last noted form of ritual in the city is especially significant for theological reflection. Be it in a giant sporting arena or in a small urban playground, the rituals of play in particular are important aspects of urban life that make for the common good. [xvi] Living out one's Christian commitments in the city is often compared in the pages of the New Testament to the work of an athlete preparing for a race, as in 1 Corinthians 9:25; running in the race, as in Hebrews 12:1 – 3; or having finished the race, as in 2 Timothy 4:7. It is not just the play of adults that is brought into metaphorical view here. Indeed, one might not find a better space in the city for theological reflection than on the playground of children, as Jesus did in Luke 7:31 – 35.

16

The point here is that sacrifice is not the only liturgical action taking place on the third altars throughout the city. Sacrifice is not at odds with playing, by any means. The training that an athlete undergoes in preparation for the arena is often seen as a form of sacrifice. In 2 Timothy 4:6 the apostle notes first that he is being poured out as a drink offering, and then in verse 7 that he has completed the race in good order. Sacrifice is not the last word in these instances, however. The sacrifice gives way to something else, something that is better suited for the playground than the battlefield.

Seeing the city as a playground rather than a battleground is clearly metaphorical. [xvii] But if one follows the logic of faith both ancient and modern, one quickly realizes with McFague that all theological thinking is metaphorical. The words of the eucharistic liturgy that takes place on the second altar, "This is my body ... This is my blood ... " are no less metaphorical than the words of the Son of Man sitting in judgment of all nations who says in Matthew 25:40 concerning the third altar, "Truly I tell you, just as you did it to one of the least of these brothers and sisters of mine, you did it to me" (NRSVUE). Being able to discern that there is more than regular bread and wine on the second of Chrysostom's altars is a critical element in traditional Catholic pastoral practice for determining whether one be allowed to partake in the eucharistic meal that is celebrated there. Being able to discern Christ elsewhere in the city where he has told us to look (Matthew 25:40) is equally important. We are invited by Christ himself not just to see the city as a playground rather than a battleground — we are invited to join him on the playground, working, playing, and celebrating together for the life of the city, for the common good.

i *John Chrysostom, "Discourse II," in* Four Discourses of Chrysostom, Chiefly on the Parable of the Rich Man and Lazarus, *trans. by F. Allen (London: Longmans, Green Reader, and Dyer, 1869), 59. See also* St John Chrysostom on Wealth and Poverty, *translated and introduced by Catherine P. Roth (Crestwood, NY: St Vladimir's Seminary Press, 1984).*

ii *The complete text of the liturgy of John Chrysostom as used today in Greek*
Orthodox churches throughout the world can be found in both English and Greek on the webpage of the Greek Orthodox Archdiocese of America, online at https://www.goarch.org/-/the-divine-liturgy-of-saint-john-chrysostom. See also David L. Frost, trans., The Divine Liturgies of Saint John Chrysostom and Saint Basil the Great *(Cambridge: Aquila Books / Institute for Orthodox Christian Studies, 2015).*

iii *Agus Widodo and Antonius Galih Arga Wiwin Aryanto,* John
Chrysostom's Commentary on the Collection for Jerusalem in Rom 15:25–32, *Verbum Vitae 40, No. 2 (2022), 552.*

iv *John Chrysostom, "Homily 20," in* Homilies of St. John Chrysostom,
Archbishop of Constantinople, on the Second Epistle of St. Paul the Apostle to the Corinthians, vol 12, Library of the Nicene and Post-Nicene Fathers of the Christian Church, Philip Schaff, general editor. (Edinburgh, T & T Clark, 1989). 374.

v *Ion Bria,* The Liturgy After the Liturgy: Mission and Witness from an
Orthodox Perspective *(Geneva: World Council of Churches, 1996). Bria notes that in Orthodox practice, there is a liturgy of preparation that takes place before the liturgy of word and sacrament, in which the deacon and priest participate. These first two liturgies then find their fulfillment in the liturgy after the liturgy, to which they both lead, which as we saw with Chrysostom entails work that seek to alleviate poverty and oppression in the world.*

vi *Maxwell E. Johnson and Stefanos Alexopoulos, Introduction to Eastern*
Christian Liturgies *(Collegeville: The Liturgical Press, 2021). The identification of the seven existing traditions or rites is found on page xv.*

vii *Anscar J. Chupungco, OSB, "A Definition of Liturgy,"* Handbook for Liturgical Studies, Volume 1: Introduction to the Liturgy *(Collegeville: The Liturgical*
Press, 1997), 3.

viii *Naphtali Lewis, "Leitourgia and Related Terms,"* Greek, Roman, and Byzantine Studies 3, No. 4 *(Fall 1960),* 175-184; 181.

ix *See Ronald L. Grimes,* Beginnings in Ritual Studies *(/ Waterloo, Canada: CreateSpace Independent Publishing Platform, 2014, 3rd edition; originally*
published Lanham, MD: University Press of America, 1982), especially chapter 1, "Interpreting Ritual in the Field," 2-18.

x *David Tracy* The Analogical Imagination: Christian Theology and the Culture of Pluralism *(New York: Crossroad Publishing, 1981).*

xi *For a detailed philosophical look at the use of analogy in Thomas Aquinas, see Ralph M. McInerny,* Aquinas and Analogy *(Washington, DC: Catholic*
University of America Press, 1998).

xii *Robert Masson, "Analogy as Higher-Order Metaphor in Aquinas," in* Divine Transcendence and Immanence in the Work of Thomas Aquinas,
edited by Harm Goris, Herwi Rikhof, and Henk Schoot (Walpole, MA: Peeters Publishers, 2009), 111–128.

xiii *Sallie McFague,* Speaking in Parables: A Study in Metaphor and Theology *(Philadelphia: Fortress Press, 1975).*

xiv *Sallie McFague,* Metaphorical Theology: Models of God in Religious Language *(Philadelphia: Fortress Press, 1982).*

xv *Mary Zournazi, "A Reflection: Kairos or the Foreignness of My Tongue,"* Life Writing 2, no. 1 (2005), 141.

xvi *On the serious work developmental that children carry out through play, see Erik H. Erikson,* Toys and Reasons: Stages in the Ritualization of
Experience *(New York: W. W. Norton & Co., 1977). On the nature of "playing" in general in the construction of meaning in human experience, see Hans-Georg Gadamer,* The Relevance of the Beautiful *(London: Cambridge University Press, 1986)..*

xvii *Dave Hillis,* Cities: Playgrounds or Battlegrounds?: Leadership Foundations' Fifty Year Journey of Social and Spiritual Renewal *(Tacoma:*
Leadership Foundation Publishing, 2014).

LISTENING TO THE CITY

Abhishek Gier

Founder and Executive Director of Catalyst
Leadership Foundation in New Delhi

Our goal should be to search for the realization of an ideal society, knowing it is a quest that always eludes humankind but one that we must compulsively seek.

Merrill Kaplan, *Philanthropist*

Anytime I recall my move to Delhi I remember my deep sense of overwhelm, bordering on paralysis, that led to an existential crisis. We have heard it sung in America that "New York is a city that never sleeps." Delhi is a city that never went to bed in the first place.

Delhi welcomes you by exhausting you. It's a city where everyone is striving to make ends meet and fighting to survive. It has created what is known as the "Delhi swagger." A kind of deliberate, defiant, and daring sashay that will not be put-off or put down. And truth be told something like it is needed with a population nearing 30 million people that can swell on any given day by another 5 million coming into the city for work. Or the more than 10 million vehicles on the road that can move one toward an ever-increasing sense of urban claustrophobia. You are constantly tempted to get emotionally, mentally, physically, and spiritually exhausted. There's a constant voice telling you to do something to survive the day. There's no rest. And if you're not careful, no play.

The sheer speed and substance of the place is also veined with delight. The streets of Delhi are a vibrant mix of culture, history, and modernity. They are bustling with people, vehicles, street vendors, and shops. The streets are lined with colorful buildings, temples, and monuments, reflecting the city's rich heritage. The narrow two-lane roads of Old Delhi are a feast for the senses, with their busy street markets, crowded food stalls, and vibrant atmosphere. These dance with the wider, tree-lined streets of New Delhi showcasing the city's colonial past, with grand government buildings, embassies, and green spaces. These physical realities are compounded by a further phenomenon: no one is from Delhi.

How could this be true, that no one is from a city of 30+ million inhabitants? Certainly, there are homes with people living in them. There are businesses that have addresses. Delhi is the home of cricket teams that are cheered for. And yet for all of these essential facts, the simple truth is that it feels like nobody is actually from Delhi. If you ask anyone, "Is Delhi where you're from?" they will have an answer that is not Delhi. You are, when push comes to shove, fending for yourself, fighting for your family, fussing about your future. The city herself does not belong to anyone. No one owns it. Everybody just uses the city for their survival or for their benefit. No one says, "I belong to Delhi." Ultimately this has the devastating effect of seeing the city as a battleground rather than a playground. It was in and from this context that the idea of Delhi being a playground, God's playground, began to emerge. But it took a while.

Similar to experiencing Delhi for the first time I still remember hearing Leadership Foundations' outlandish idea of seeing your respective city as God's playground rather than a battleground. Both Angie (my wife and co-leader of our local LF chapter, Catalyst) and I, not dissimilar to Abraham upon hearing the news that at he and his wife's old age, would be having a child, laughed. And our laughter produced questions. How, in God's name, we wondered, do we even begin to see this teeming, turbulent, and tempestuous city of Delhi as a playground?

In my conversations with people around the city, I started discovering that there are a lot of people who, although they initially say they don't belong to Delhi, eventually fall in love with the city without even knowing it. They care for the city. And they don't have any avenue to actually display that love. We started asking questions as a group. What does it mean to be a part of a city? Why are we here? We started thinking about the city as a playground. We thought about another metaphor of the city—that of the prostitute and the bride from the book of Revelation in the Bible. Are we using the city, or can we love and care for and stay with the city?

What we have learned is that if one has any hope of seeing their city become a playground it begins with behaving as though it is yours. In order to do this, we have to be humanly proximate, we have to listen to the city, and we have to be relational with each other.

While being able to describe what is taking place in the city of Delhi and articulating a simple way forward through the complexity is required, it can never take the place of being humanly proximate. As G.K. Chesterton stated so beautifully about how cities grow great,

> *If men/women loved [their city] as mothers love children, arbitrarily, because it is THEIRS, [their city] in a year or two might be fairer than Florence. Some readers will say that this is a mere fantasy. I answer that this is the actual history of humankind. This, as a fact, is how cities did grow great.*

To do this we must be close enough to hear the voice of the city. We have to attune our spiritual ears. This becomes a decidedly emotional and spiritual exercise, but one that is needed if we are to engage our cities as playgrounds. If one does this with any kind of consistency what begins to disappear is fear, the primary enemy of doing good work in a city.

I have now lived in Delhi most of my life, and even though I have immersed myself in her, I'm not ashamed to say that I still don't know Delhi completely. I am still learning new things every day. I'm still learning about new communities coming into Delhi. I am still learning about communities who have lived in Delhi for 100 years but have not been visible.

Cities are living, breathing organisms and we have to hear their voices. Cities talk back. They communicate. Delhi is a noisy city. I had to tune my spiritual ears to hear that voice. It's an emotional and spiritual exercise. And then it becomes our responsibility to respond to what we hear. If it is pain we hear, as I have heard, it is our responsibility to try to heal that pain. Often healing is not within our capacity so we then ask, how do we bring that pain to the forefront to make sure others hear that pain?

In Delhi, we are nothing if not close to each other. But it is easy to fall into the trap of being near each other without being with each other. People, regardless of station in life, are moved, motivated, and molded by the relationality that surrounds them and only, afterwards, our rationality. It will be the parent, coach, mentor, friend, colleague who has far greater effect on who we become then any kind of rational discourse or dispute.

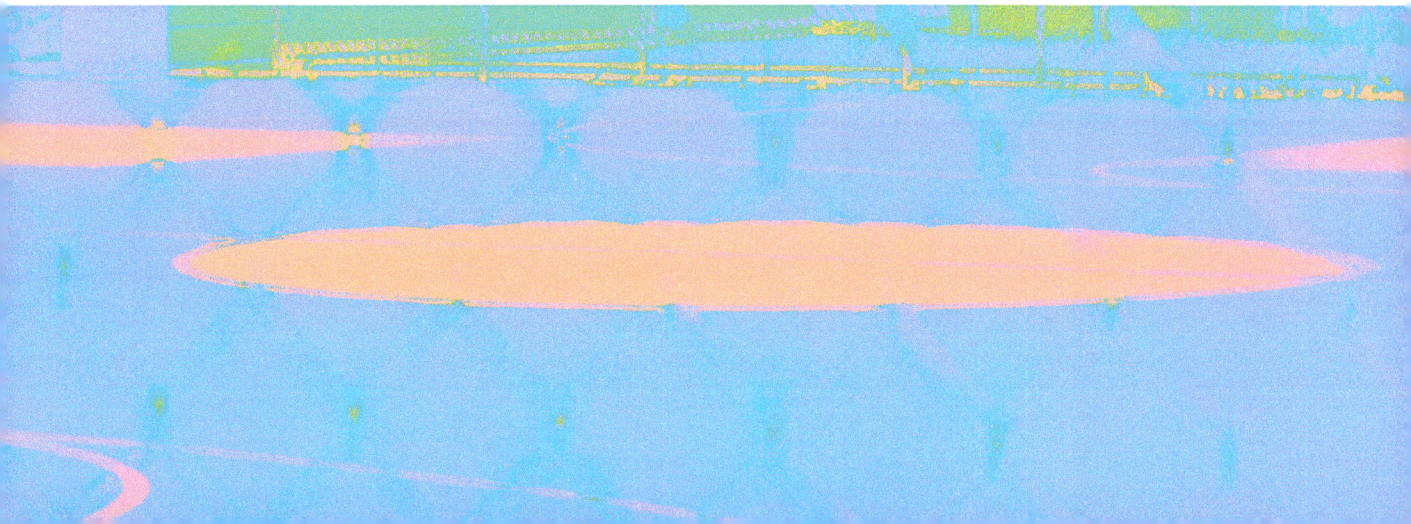

For a city to become more like a playground rather than a battleground, it will depend on women and men becoming present to people in their respective contexts who take them and all the dimensions of their life in considerate and compassionate ways. Simply put, and what the Catalyst Leadership Foundation has done, is deploy women and men who, in the heavy traffic of our city, first sit with our brothers and sisters and then act. And in our work, that may mean passing the baton to someone else who can take a program further than we could alone. This is only done by listening to the voice of the city and engaging with those we have built relationships with. We need an expression of leadership that sees the big picture and as a result is less swayed by the immediate.

22

One program that Catalyst Leadership Foundation ran was called Critical Care Center. We've worked for many years helping to rescue women and girls who were being trafficked between India and Nepal. We learned that 70% of those rescued have been rescued before. Once rescued, these women and girls were being sent home and back to the same cycle. The voice of the city was telling us that there are thousands of Nepalese girls being brought into the city and abused. You need to do something about it. This is when we developed the Critical Care Center to rescue, rehabilitate, bring perpetrators to justice, and get compensation to survivors. There is no dearth of trafficking rescue organizations, but these victims were being re-cycled through the trafficking industry.

One of the reasons was that the law required a rescued child to be repatriated in their home country within 15 days. That is not enough time to address trauma, to stabilize them emotionally and psychologically, and to find a safe place to return them to. We lobbied the government for a change in the law and explained to lawmakers that using a 3–6-month stabilization process would save enormous resources for the city. Eventually, we were successful and now they've become advocates of what we've done, which gives us the authority to now go to other

organizations and tell them this works. We had success but every year, there are probably 100,000 girls being trafficked between India and Nepal. We do not have the capacity to deal with that as a singular organization and so are committed to bringing other leaders of good faith and good will together.

We ran a home for about 30 girls providing those key stabilization services. That is not enough to meet the need. So, we decided to change the Critical Care Center to a critical care service, which shared what we learned and developed and passed it on to other homes that are serving survivors of trafficking. In passing it on to others our collective impact was magnified 1,000 percent. And that's where we see the city as a playground again. We are playing a game where we are happy to pass on what we have and see the victory happening.

In pursuit of the idyllic, we can become impatient and feel what we are actually seeing is a plague-ground, strewn with dirt, blood, weapons and death. It takes courage to stand in the plague-ground, making yourself vulnerable to the dangers, listening to the voices, and eventually starting to clean up and build the playground. What is required is something Eugene Peterson called "a long obedience in the same direction." It will be this quality that will help us weather those dark and desperate days as we move forward. This has certainly been the case in Delhi.

While still overwhelmed by the big idea of Delhi becoming God's playground, we are cautiously hopeful as we compulsively seek. By getting proximate, listening to the city, and leaning into relationship, we are ever so slowly seeing Delhi emerge as a place of destination rather than destitution; promise instead of peril and; hope instead of horror.

Dr.

DAVE HILLIS

Rev.

JEN BAILEY

Author and Founder and Executive
Director of the Faith Matters Network

In Conversation

Dave:

As you know, one of the charisms that LF has been given and attempted to steward is that we try to see the city as God's playground rather than a battleground. I want to ask you about an important piece of that — seeing. How would it change the way one might do theology for example, or sociology or for practitioners on the ground if they saw things through that prism? How important is *seeing* in ministry?

Jen:

You know, we talk a lot about the notion of 'hearing the call,' right? That you're called by God, it's something you hear. I would argue that the true call to ministry is an act of metaphorical seeing, being able to pay attention in a very real way to the world as it is, but having the sort of spark of moral imagination, to envision the world as it could be. In the Christian tradition, we might talk about that as what it means to help manifest the kingdom of God here on Earth. And so, when I think about the art of seeing, it's both about paying attention to how God is showing us and speaking to us in a season. I think the gift of the metaphor of sight is once you see, you can't unsee.

It also feels like a moment of revelation. And I think in these times, those of us who are called to do the work of ministry, are being called to see with new eyes, but not to avert our eyes from that which might be uncomfortable, from that which is painful, that which is broken, that which might push us, that might fundamentally transform us in our theology. There's something in the context of ministry that opens a gateway to potential transformation, if, and it feels like a big if, we are willing to be in a state of humility, to recognize that our way of seeing may not be the only way. That indeed, God's call and vision is bigger than anything that any one person can imagine.

D: I love the way you articulate that notion of both being able to see what could be but not averting our eyes from what is. What would you say, are some of the practices or maybe disciplines that are needed in order to live in that tension?

J: There's something about being deeply rooted in the lineage of your spiritual tradition, and the practices that have sustained people in that tradition. Not just now, but always. Whether that be practices of prayer, or ways of knowing and being community. What I feel like is really clear to me is that that work of discernment doesn't happen alone but must be performed in community. And that while there's certainly a deep value in things like solitude and private study of text and reading of theology, and the practice of being with oneself, there's something in these times that I believe is calling for us to be able to balance that notion with a more collectivist mindset.

D: What does that look like for you?

26

J: For me, that looks like everything from showing up and leading the weekly prayer line for my church and viewing and petitioning the prayers of the people to more sacramental duties. Sometimes it's in the more mundane ways of just being present for folks at church meetings and delivering gift baskets for the sick and the shut in. There's something in the art of community that feels important to name. And even the work of being in community is a discipline. Because people are people, y'all, and they will get on your nerves!

D: A hearty Amen to that! As we think about community, both our immediate communities that we build or choose, and the larger communities that we inhabit with others across differences, in order to have that collectivist mindset you mentioned, what do you think needs to be in place in order to cultivate that?

J: What immediately comes to mind is the concept of covenant. What are the covenants that we are making collectively and with communities that ensure the thriving of all? Profit is always going to be a motivation for people. And enhancing one's bottom line is always going to be a motivation for people. But what we're inviting people to do in thinking about the city as a playground that allows for the flourishing and thriving of all, is really entering into a covenant or relationship with all members of a community, most particularly those who have been abused and disinvested in by policies that don't serve them and, truth be told, that have served to push them to the margin. And I think that covenant has to be one of the tools we employ that outlines the ethics through which we operate and must be co-created. It can't just be you people in a space making up a covenant for the poor. It needs to be co-written. And in some cases, the lead authors ought to be people who have been most impacted by decisions that have had generational consequences for their families and communities. At least theologically, starting with a covenant — what we mean and how we are committed to one another — allows us a basis through which to spark imagination about what is possible together, but also holds ourselves accountable and holds one another accountable when we began operating outside of those pre-conditions that we set forward.

D: Absolutely. I love that idea of a covenant. Without a covenant, without rules, the playground or our cities, can be tough places. Thinking now about literal playgrounds, those that operate well, there is always the playground monitor of some sort, right? Teachers, parents. The person that makes sure that the bully doesn't get to own the slide by himself, or that certain kids are able to access the monkey bars.

28

J: Yes. The first thing that came to mind was wise elders, the wisdom keepers of the community. The abuelas, the tias, the grannies, the mee-maws. There's something important about that role and we often cast aside our wisdom keepers and elders to our detriment. But bringing them into a space of holding for our communities, which they naturally do anyway, as one that works in concert with others, to help play that monitor function and to help us take stock of where we are and to make sure things don't go off the rails.

As I think about my own city, Nashville, like many cities in the United States it is a desperately and deeply gentrifying community. Sekou Franklin, who is an organizer and professor at Middle Tennessee State University that studies cities and urban communities, says that Nashville runs the risk of becoming a playground for the rich and a graveyard for the poor. That analogy has stuck with me. I think that metaphor of the city as a playground — on the one hand, what I love about it is its invitation to play and imagine, very practically helping people envision a different way of being collectively together in these times. And at the same time, I'm curious about the question of the playground for whom and to what ends. I'm holding both the possibilities of the metaphor and what it means to develop a theology that is inclusive of a wide variety of people and seeing those people as active agents co-creating what that playground could be. And also, the tension that exists when we see the way in which, unchecked, the intentionality behind what we are doing could potentially serve only a few versus serving the well-being of all. In a word, a graveyard.

D: That is well said. And you're putting your finger on something that has troubled me, probably for the better part of my whole ministry career. The notion that, we're in a community and some really positive things are happening that makes the community a place of possible flourishing, but then becomes a place ripe for gentrification. And if we take the playground metaphor seriously, it is going to inevitably begin to generate power which is the very thing people will fight over. How do you think this way of seeing might do to the shape of power?

J: I've come to understand that power is not innately bad. But that it's the way that power is wielded and shared that makes the difference. What does it look like to build a playground in which everyone has a role and a contribution to its design? So that as we're thinking about metaphorical slide placement or the monkey bars or whatever it might be, we have a diverse cacophony of voices that are contributing and helping us think about everything from access to accessibility. Voices that are helping us think about who ultimately the playground is serving and removing the gatekeeping that can happen. The city as a playground would be an invitation for people to see themselves as powerful beings and would model through the creation of that metaphorical playground what it looks like to share power, and what it looks like for everyone's genius to be acknowledged, allowing space for people's gifts to rise up and be utilized in the creation and functioning of that playground. 🏐

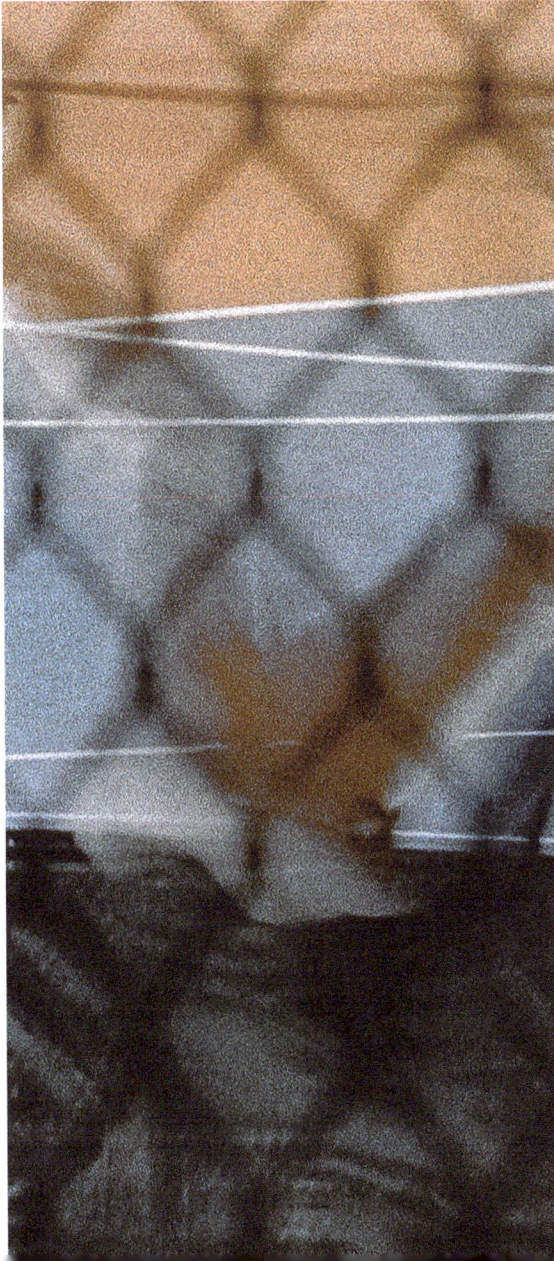

two.

two.

32

A Playground of Institutions

CURTIS CHANG

Author and Founding Executive
Director of Redeeming Babel

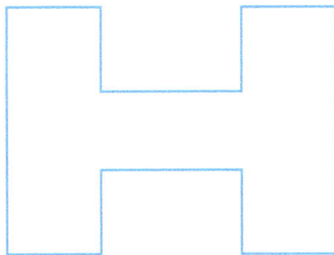

Human beings work and play. Christian theology is tasked with making sense of these core human activities, especially by asking the question, "How do humans pursue these activities as bearers of the image of God?"

Too often, however, this examination has conceived of the human primarily as the individual and neglected the institution. For example, the Faith and Work theological movement has historically examined questions of work from this narrowly privatized lens: "To which vocation am I personally called? How do I act ethically in my particular job? How do I share the gospel with my co-worker? What does it mean for me to pursue excellence?" As theologians, pastors, and lay people, we generally neglect examining the spiritual nature of our secular organizations: the corporation, the small business, the nonprofit or government agency.[i]

Yet the vast majority of Christians spend their lives working in and for such institutional beings. Their work lives are defined by advancing the aims of these organizations. If theology does not provide them with an understanding of how God's purpose connects to these organizations, how could they possibly have a robust sense of purpose in their work lives?

IF CHRISTIANS ARE TO FULLY GRASP GOD'S PURPOSE FOR THEIR LIVES OF PLAY, THEY NEED TO SEE THEMSELVES AS NOT JUST INDIVIDUALS, BUT ALSO AS INSTITUTIONAL BEINGS.

In the same manner, any theological consideration of human play—especially in the urban context—requires correcting for this blind spot. If Christians are to fully grasp God's purpose for their lives of play, they need to see themselves as not just individuals, but also as institutional beings. It is here—our acknowledged blind spot toward institutions—that the metaphor of city as playground becomes important. Through this metaphor we are provided a perspective to not only consider the individual but, and this is essential, the landscape by which the individual largely plays and makes meaning: institutions.

How Do Humans Play?

The metaphor of the city as playground envisions human beings engaged in play. But who exactly are the players? Solely the individual?

Consider me—a middle-aged male living in San Jose, California and looking for new forms of recreation. In particular I am interested in rekindling my Little League love of baseball but in the more athletically accessible form of adult softball. Immediately I am confronted with the collective aspect of most forms of human play. I cannot pitch to myself. I cannot hit a ball that could be fielded. I cannot throw to myself. To play softball I must be on a team that plays against an opposing team.

While some human play can be conducted by individuals—think of a solo violinist "playing" her instrument by herself—most human play involves playing with others. Even the exceptions prove this rule: the solo violinist may practice alone but the range of musical glory found in Bach or Beethoven symphonies will remain out of her grasp. Similarly, I can go to a batting cage to practice alone by hitting against a pitching machine. But the fulfillment of that practice—say, crushing a game winning homer to left field—is entirely out of my reach outside a collective identity (and may be out of my reach in any case, but that's a story of my athletic—not existential—limitations).

How will I find my playmates? In some distant contexts of human history like a close-knit rural village, I could informally find, recruit, and organize other individuals to play together at a given time. But in a city, it almost certainly requires I adopt a series of institutional identities. I must join a formally constituted team in a particular adult softball league organized by the San Jose Department of Parks, Recreation and Neighborhood Services.

But the institutional nature of play doesn't stop there. It has been years since I played, and I no longer own a softball bat. I cannot craft one by myself. I will have to shop at Dick's Sporting Goods, which depends on the Teamsters Union to receive shipments from the Easton bat manufacturer, which in turn relies on unionized labor to work on raw materials that ultimately originated from the Alcoa mining conglomerate. Consider other expressions of human play. How many do not rely on an analogous network of institutions to produce its basic instruments?

Properly equipped, I show up at our first game. This being an adult league, the weekday games take place at night. This means our play is dependent on the cooperative interaction between the Parks Department and Pacific Gas and Electric to illuminate the field. Between innings, we sip from the water fountain in our dugout connected to a complex infrastructure maintained by San Jose Water. As the game wears on into the night, we feel safe because the San Jose Police Department sends patrols through the park periodically.

Such complex webs of organizational interdependencies define a human city in far more durable fashion than any individual or individual relationships. Indeed, if the collective beings I listed were to suddenly disappear, the city would soon cease to function, much less play.

I could go on, but the point is obvious: human play is a profoundly institutional activity. Indeed, the fact that humans play *institutionally* is one of the qualities that distinguishes humans from animals, much more than the sheer activity of play itself. Humans are not the only beings that play. Dogs will together chase after balls in a playful manner. But dogs don't form ball chasing leagues with a sign-up process, registration fees, published rules of play, designated umpires, and team uniforms.

The capacity for institutional life seems to be a uniquely human trait. Animals may form collectives like flocks and colonies, but these non-human collective entities lack the qualities that distinguish an *institution* from a *collective*: traits such as official structure, defined roles, membership via qualities beyond blood, and most of all, self-conscious identity. I am not an expert in the study of the primates most genetically closest to us, but to the best of my knowledge, a tribe of chimpanzees has never collected dues for a team uniform bearing their tribal name.

The act of naming—the granting of identity in a self-aware manner—is a distinctive trait of human beings. The Genesis narrative describes this naming activity as the first assignment given to human beings, one which marks their distinction from other non-human beings. Our softball team follows this pattern. The city initially constituted us only as "Team B," but the first agenda item of our first team meeting was to come up with a name. The second item was deciding who would order monogrammed t-shirts to announce the "The Giants" have indeed come into being.

Every human institution comes into being in a similar fashion. When a corporation charters itself, when a new law forms a new government agency, or when a small business hangs a shingle, a profoundly human activity is taking place. Humans are naming themselves, doing so in a fully self-aware fashion, and bringing into existence a new form of collective humanity. When organizations come into being, fundamental qualities of human being-ness are being enacted.

Tool Versus Being

When I propose to other theologians that the institution participates in the spiritual qualities of being human, some will object almost viscerally. Our contemporary culture suffers from an ingrained suspicion of institutions, and this suspicion seemingly has taken root among theologians.

Some of these skeptics argue that humans create organizations to enable human activity but that organizations are not themselves *beings*. They insist institutions are human *tools*, not human *beings*. In this view, the naming of our softball team is thus much more akin to me naming my favorite hammer than it is to naming my child.

But what is the basis for automatically excluding the human institution from participating in the human at the existential level of *being*? Why should we categorize an organization as a mere tool? A hammer is obviously just a tool created by humans because it is composed of metal and rubber: non-human ingredients joined together by purely chemical and mechanical relationships. But San Jose Water is composed of human beings joined together in living activity and relationships. In their essence, human institutions are just that: *human*.

36

If we toss a hammer into the trash overnight, we only lose a thing. If we demolish San Jose Water overnight, the cascading losses are profoundly human in nature: of meaningful employment and financial provision for workers, of relationships between colleagues, of provision of the water necessary for human flourishing in the city, of the responsible stewardship of creation for this region.

The moral language and expectations we apply to human institutions further demonstrate their nature as beings, and not just as tools. Suppose San Jose Water failed to adequately purify the water supplied to our park because managers and workers were systematically bribed by local companies to look the other way at industrial pollution. If our team got sick, we would apply moral language to this failure. We would claim that we were *betrayed*. In other words, we would locate this institution in the moral and spiritual narrative of human fallenness. If a hammer broke, we might decry its flaws but would not use such moral and spiritual language.

Recognizing human institutions as an expression of humanity does not mean entirely granting an organization the exact *identical* spiritual status, we grant an individual. We acknowledge different forms of human being besides the individual, such as the married couple, the family, or the church. Each possess qualities of being with spiritual and moral values that differ from the individual (and from each other). But they are all recognized as fully human.

The individual is a far more precious expression of humanity than an institution. Yes, if San Jose Water were to be shut down and cease existence overnight as an institution, there would be real human losses; but those losses would still be much less weighty than, say, if a horrible accident caused the hospitalization of an individual member. An institutional life is not the same as an individual life and is "lesser than" in a variety of meaningful ways. A set of spiritual meanings are reserved for the individual.

However, remember the converse: a set of spiritual meanings are reserved for the institution. As the examples of softball and symphonies illustrate, a wealth of human capacities is only made possible via institutions. Consider any other human achievement today that conveys the Biblical notion of *glory* that is reserved for humanity, whether it be in the realm of literature, architecture, education, or technology. Take away the publishing firm, the construction company, the university, and the start-up. Practically all those achievements disappear. In other words, an individual existing — and playing — alone is in many ways "lesser than" those engaged in organizational life.

The truth that humans need organizations to fully reflect God's purposes explains why the early church responded to Jesus' death and resurrection with a creative surge of new types of institutions. As the Biblical scholar Kavin Rowe has documented, early Christians invented the orphanage, the hospital, the university, and more. These new institutions transformed urban life in the Roman empire.[ii]

The city as *playground* metaphor is a rich opportunity. Fully mining this metaphor for insights into God's purpose for humanity requires that we consider the human institution and not just the individual. In play — and in work — the institution matters deeply. And it matters at the level of intrinsic being and not just as an instrumental tool.

This means that we urban Christians are called to invest meaningfully in the wellbeing and dignity of our city's institutions. We instinctively recognize that we do not look at an individual neighbor and just ask, "What can I get out of this person for my benefit?" Rather, we know that precisely because this individual participates in the human experience and thus bears the image of God, we are called to serve, forgive, and love that being.

Christians are called to adopt a similar posture towards our urban institutions. Those companies, government agencies, nonprofits, civic associations, and other organizations are profoundly human beings. As beings, they matter to God. All of them matter — even the softball team. ⊕

---

i *For an excellent exception to this rule, see: Andy Crouch, in* Playing God: Redeeming the Gift of Power *(Downers Grove, IL: IVP Books, 2013), pp. 169 – 206. For a seminal analysis on the overall paucity of institutional thinking afflicting all disciplines, see: Hugh Heclo,* On Thinking Institutionally *(Oxford: Oxford Univ. Press, 2013).*
ii *Christopher Kavin Rowe, "4," in* Christianity's Surprise: A Sure and Certain Hope *(Nashville: Abingdon Press, 2020).*

The Church
AS THE
Playground
OF
Creation

DR. LUKE BRETHERTON

Author, Theologian and Robert E. Cushman
Distinguished Professor of Moral &
Political Theology at Duke University

The artist L. S. Lowry spent his life painting scenes from the urban, industrial heartlands of Northwest England. His 1949 picture *A Football Match* depicts a landscape of factories in the foreground of which a crowd gathers around a football match. This game is not imposed on or alien to the industrialized world it takes place in. Lowry's portrait of this game is neither nostalgic nor utopian. He depicts a real world. Yet the play we see is in, but not of that world. Rather, even as it emerges from that world, it transcends it. The play transforms it—if only for a moment—from a realm of drudgery, backbreaking toil, and exploitation into one of solidarity, freedom, and fun.

In contemplating this scene of play set among modernity's dark satanic mills, Lowry invites us to consider the different ways of being human the factory and the football match represent. His picture asks us to imagine other ways of forming a common life, ways that reconstitute the possibilities currently available to those that modern industrialized economies and urban life offer. Lowry portrays a way of being together born out of serious play rather than grinding labour. It is a form of life that humanizes and liberates rather than alienates and exploits. The church as itself a form of deep play should do the same.

Gathering for worship offers a moment of contemplation of that which lies beyond the immediate needs and demands of forming and sustaining a common life here and now. In doing so, the church insists that in the last analysis not everything is reducible to either economics or politics. Without such times, the world of making and politicking dominates every aspect of life, including our imaginations. A direct consequence of our political economy becoming the only and all-encompassing point of reference is that instead of political and economic systems being a means to serve human flourishing, humans are instrumentalized to serve political and economic systems. As with the industrialized world Lowry depicted, our political economy becomes an idol upon whose alter is sacrificed humans and all that makes life precious.

In our world, like in Lowry's, especially in a western context, the state and the market want to dominate us. The state wants us as a subject and the market wants us as a consumer. Both want highly atomized individuals who can be easily moved about, monitored, and controlled.

42

IT IS ONLY IN THE GATHERING WITH OTHERS, IN A NON–STATE BASED AND NON–MARKET BASED MODE OF ASSOCIATION, THAT THE INDIVIDUAL HAS ANY POWER AND AGENCY TO PURSUE THEIR OWN PURPOSES AND GOALS.

Without the support and solidarity of others, we are naked before the unilateral forces of market and state. In this context, the gathering of the church as a form of deep play generates both the fellowship and the capacity needed to act with and for others. This, of course, makes the church a threat to the market and the state. Under authoritarian regimes, the church is made to either serve the state or persecuted. In other contexts, the church is co-opted by market and state forces so as to serve their ends.

The church, by being the church, should hold open times and spaces for wonder, prayer, rest, festivity, and play. These are ways to regenerate the human spirit and embody the reality that humans do not live by bread alone. Worship as a form of deep play is not leisure but an existential necessity if life together is to remain humane.

Congregations are constituted by people who do not come together primarily for either commercial, state-directed transactions, or the necessities of family life. Instead, they form institutions through which to worship God, receive creation in the form of bread and wine as a gift to be shared, and care for each other as those who bear the image of God. Without such institutions, there are few places through which to resist commodification by the market, instrumentalization — and sometimes brutal repression — by the state, and over-determination by the demands of family life. In short, if we have nowhere to sit together free from governmental, commercial, or even familial imperatives, we have no shared spaces in which to take the time to receive each other and the world around us as a gift to be delighted in rather a resource to be used.

Historically, the church was the vanguard of creating holidays, festivals, liturgical seasons, and other ways of organizing life together to ensure times and spaces for wonder, prayer, rest, and festivity. In doing so, it created times and spaces—for example, cathedrals, feast days, and sabbath keeping—to ensure neither the family, the state, nor the market had total control over the shape of life. It thereby resisted and contested the inevitable drive of immanent political, economic, and social processes to make gods of themselves and thereby determine the ultimate meaning and purpose of life.

The challenge of the modern world is that, in the name of being secular (and thereby emancipated from the dead hand of tradition and religion), we came to view the totalization of political, economic, and social life as liberation rather than as an enslavement to false gods. The demands of state, market, and family are not the sum total of what it means to be human. What it means to be human is not defined by the ceaseless demand to make money, administer bureaucratic and technological systems, and keep everyone fed and housed. The struggle for the church today is to re-sacralise life together through restoring times and spaces for wonder, prayer, rest, and festivity; in other words, for serious play. Echoing Lowry's vision of the football match amid sites of industrial extraction, we reinhabit the city of God when the earthly city

is rendered a field of play. This can be as simple as saying grace before a meal and thereby recognizing that the food that keeps me alive is first and foremost a gift to give thanks for and not a resource to be used without any consideration of the soil and hands that made this food possible.

Through inhabiting saint's days, Advent, Christmas, Lent, Easter, and gathering Sunday by Sunday, the church cultivates a hunger and thirst for ways of life that do not seek in economic, political, or social processes the sole source of meaning and purpose. In doing these things it proclaims that the last word about being human is not that we are utility maximisers, administrative units, consumers, or entirely subject to the obligations of kith and kin. Different cultures will give greater or lesser emphasis on one or other of these. But no matter the cultural context, the witness of the church is to refuse the totalization of any earthly time and space as the be all and end all of everything. In doing so the church comes into conflict and threatens all imminent programs for remaking the world in our own image rather than receiving creation as a time and place in which we discover, play with, and live out ways of being alive that image our creator. In short, if the church is fulfilling her vocation, it becomes a place where humans learn what it means to inhabit cities as sites of redemptive play that brings blessings to others. ⊕

What Do You See?

REV. DR. RANDY WHITE

Author, Founder of the Center for Community
Transformation, Leadership Foundation of
Fresno

We *think* we see. Like the blind man partially healed, having never seen a man, we mistake one thing for something else we've never seen — a tree. And in our work in the city, having become accustomed to partial sight, we have convinced ourselves that only a quick glance is necessary to know the situation there, and what would make for flourishing, or what the Bible calls *shalom.* We read the first paragraph but not the article, smell the food cooking but don't stay for the whole meal. We already know how it will read, how it will taste. In the city we see the yard full of weeds but not the flowerbox in the window, the vitriolic headline but not the civil dialogue at the meeting, the neglect and violence of the neighborhood, but not the heroic grandmother cooking for God-knows-how-many neighborhood kids.

This Looking Business is Risky

How easy it is to slide into a comfortable sloth when trying to understand our city, avoiding the discipline required of true sight. Annie Dillard helped me realize long ago that there are two ways of seeing, certainly in nature, but in cities as well. The first is a form of acute observation, attention to minute detail, where we "analyze and pry" and "study…a square foot at a time."[i] Though she will acknowledge how crucial this approach is, she believes there is another way of seeing that we must wait for, be available for — a sight that simply materializes and surprises, and perhaps even, overpowers. "This looking business is risky," she says.[ii] Sometimes it is illuminated by the kind of light we cannot ourselves produce, the light that simply falls. I will come back to this second way of seeing, but before I do, we must not sidestep the first when trying to see the city in a fresh way. We will indeed need to do the hard work of examination and focus on the things that impair our seeing. It is just that as we do, we can't stay there, in the minutia, or we fall for the trap C.S. Lewis warned of, thinking that the dust floating in a dazzling shaft of light is the point, rather than *where* the light comes from or what you can see *by* the light. As Lewis observed, all-too-often, "[We can] go on explaining a thing without knowing what it is."[iii]

There is a whole lot of that going on — explaining without knowing — among leaders seeking the peace of the city, which is why we so often fall into the cynicism of seeing cities as battlegrounds rather than playgrounds: a place where joy and laughter thrive, where interests can be negotiated, and a mutually beneficial future is built. As it is so often it is our factual examination of the city where our eyesight becomes the problem.

The Fog of War

Without a clear and accurate assessment of our city, the murkiness we are left with becomes problematic. Our vision is clouded and blurred. It creates fear and even paralysis. Cataracts can't be corrected with new glasses. It often requires divine surgery — in the case of St. Paul, scales falling from his eyes. And to make matters worse, all sorts of "doctors" appear to tell us what's wrong with our sight. Activists with their one urgent cause in mind, or their one approved methodology, or their better theology, or their most enlightened and cutting-edge terminology. They will pronounce the cure, and publicly declare whether your agency is on board with it. Toxic activism is so good at describing the problem, it infects everyone, and the problem looms so large that the only answer that anyone can see is to get more resources and power. Activism at its best empowers people through the vehicle of love. But at its worst, it depends on the problem being persistent, and those on crusade can become bullies on the playground of the city. The result is not more clarity, just more fog, and it is the fog of war.

47

The Antidote of Other Eyes

But there is a more common condition. The majority of faith-based practitioners I have walked with over forty years all struggle with the same thing—nearsightedness. While we begin building a city-wide coalition, going to meetings where we share aspirations, develop joint vision statements (it is true, we see better together), and agree on a plan, ultimately, there is the pressure to submit to our boards, our funders, our volunteers, even to public opinion. There is a strong, gravitational pull to our specialties, and ultimately, our silos. We end up with a myopic concentration on survival. Those few able to link their specialties to other entities in the community in order to form friendships, joint projects and more collaborative efforts, find a greater ability to see beyond their immediate needs to a preferred future and a way to get there. Together.

During the early months of COVID we had conversations with 33 small faith-based non-profits/CBOs in our city of Fresno, California which revealed real fear about their survival. Our university-based Center for Community Transformation raised $100,000 on their behalf to help them bridge the first few months until they could adjust their strategies and brought them together to listen. We were worried too, but didn't take any of that donated money, out of friendship. The faith-based partnerships in our city grew stronger for it. The challenge of COVID helped us operationalize the multitude of eyes available to watch each other's backs.

Slightly Off

My city has a reputation for collaboration, a pragmatic outgrowth sprouting from the soil of our despair from previous decades where all the indicators of individual and community health were going in the wrong direction. But even in this environment that we have worked hard to cultivate, our vision can become askew. Sometimes, when we look, instead of seeing the clear edge of what is causing disruption and pain in a community, our vision unwisely shifts to the behavior itself. The fuzzy effect is the same as a slow lens trying to capture a body in motion; it leaves only a mystifying smear. Catholic priest, Father Ben Beltran who ministers among a scavenger community in the Smoky Mountain garbage dump on the outskirts of Manila, Philippines, taught me that those who would see the city most clearly must understand it at a more foundational level than the mere behaviors and needs we are seeing. We must see its *civitas*, what it is known for, what informs its reputation, and how it conducts itself. We must see it at the level of its *urbs*, how geography affects relationships and services and equity. But most importantly, we must see its *anima*, what it is that moves and animates it, i.e., the assumptions and unconscious universe of its residents.[iv] Without these lenses we lose the clear edge of reality, of what informs behavior, and the best we can do is sort through a mismatched set of Band-Aids. Father Beltran's deep dive into the identity of those living in the Smoky Mountain garbage-picker community led inevitably to working with residents on a housing solution to replace their shacks, on microenterprise approaches to generate other income, and to youth investments in cultural arts to celebrate the imago dei in every resident.

Kaleidoscope: Scintillating Scotoma

Every once in a while, I go half blind. Try saying that at dinner one night. It's a temporary condition that happens to me occasionally, usually accompanied by a slight headache. A jagged kaleidoscope appears and grows into the form of a crescent and obscures my vision. It was concerning at first, but I have learned to recognize it, and usually it goes away in 20 minutes with a little rest and ibuprofen. This kaleidoscope appears in the city as well, when the latest urgent problem dazzles, takes center stage, prevents me from seeing anything else. And it can last quite a bit longer. At the height of a decade-long, city-wide, collaborative effort to build a next-generation onramp to help emerging leaders find their place in seeking the shalom of our city, drama took over, and cut the legs out from under the carefully constructed movement. Both generational and ethnic differences sparked, and after one final, tumultuous event, we all took our game balls, left the playground, and went home. It dominated my vision for a year, crushed my spirit, and sent me into a place of fear. In the aftermath I could scarcely see that the bare roots of healing had already been planted and that good things would again sprout. It took considerable time for my sight to return, but now, before me, are multiple sprigs of beauty emerging from ashes.

Sunrise: A Seeing That Comes From Letting Go

In the end the challenge for those of us who view every city as God's *playground* rather than a *battleground* is that we must choose to *let sight come* and place ourselves in a *position* to receive it. By far, the default, inevitable, and one might say easier place from which to view the city is from our doorstep and our newsfeed — it is the vast flow of a city's problems, sins, treacheries, needs, emergencies, rivalries — akin to what Dillard calls "the muddy river of trash and trivia."[v] A little harder, is the position along the riverbank, panning for the golden nuggets of a city's beauty and strength embedded in the stream. These are the raw materials needed to build a playground available to all.

And yet, even this is not the whole story. If playground is the goal, it is also the means to get there. When uniting a city for transformation, what is needed most is a movement of friends, friends who have learned how to play together. Friends who can celebrate small victories and forgive the inevitable gaffs. Friends who show up hoping there will be enough players to form a team, and who take care of the batter's box. Friends who arrive early, who step into the bright beam of the sunrise and instinctively turn to each other exclaiming, "How beautiful!" because there is more joy in the telling than in the seeing. Perhaps there is "another kind of seeing that involves a letting go,"[vi] Dillard says. For us, could it be letting go of expectations, of turfdoms, and of having all the right answers, and instead, working for and anticipating together, as friends, the surprise, and the gift of shalom? Perhaps, together we can agree that we "cannot cause light; the most [we] can do is try to put [ourselves] in the path of its beam."[vii] In my older age, that's the light on the playground I show up to everyday. ⊕

49

i Dillard, Annie, Pilgrim at Tinker Creek *(Harper Perennial Modern Classics, 2013), p. 10.*
ii Ibid, pg. 6
iii C.S. Lewis, "Meditation in a Toolshed" in God in the Dock *(Grand Rapids: Eerdmans, 1998, pp. 212–215.)*
iv Beltran, Benigno, The Christology of the Inarticulate *(Divine Word Press, 1987)*
v Dillard, pg. 10
vi Ibid, pg. 10
vii Ibid, pg. 11

The Power OF Metaphor: Cultivating A Playful Heart

ROMANITA HAIRSTON

CEO of the M.J. Murdock Charitable Trust

THIS IS WHAT THE LORD SAYS: "I WILL RETURN TO ZION AND DWELL IN JERUSALEM. THEN JERUSALEM WILL BE CALLED THE FAITHFUL CITY, AND THE MOUNTAIN OF THE LORD ALMIGHTY WILL BE CALLED THE HOLY MOUNTAIN."

THIS IS WHAT THE LORD ALMIGHTY SAYS: "ONCE AGAIN MEN AND WOMEN OF RIPE OLD AGE WILL SIT IN THE STREETS OF JERUSALEM, EACH OF THEM WITH CANE IN HAND BECAUSE OF THEIR AGE. THE CITY STREETS WILL BE FILLED WITH BOYS AND GIRLS PLAYING THERE."

-ZECHARIAH 8:3-5

In this season of deep polarization and division where the prophetic voice of the church can have a tone of judgement and even disdain, Zechariah's prophetic voice is not only strikingly different, but also critically important. Zechariah does not shy away from bringing to light the real issues. After giving the people of Israel a very frank accounting of their issues in the prior chapters, the tone changes significantly, demonstrating that the emerging play-filled city is not to be imagined as some fairy-tale or faraway land. Rather, it is real change, transformation, and renewal of the current context.

Zechariah's words are comforting words for our communities. While seeing the city as playground might strike up visions of New York, Chicago, Los Angeles, and other major metropolitan places, it is important to realize that Zechariah is talking to the children of Israel about their community. For Jerusalem, the realization of a play-filled city was connected to the restoration of a positive reputation, successful social and political administration, abundant and plentiful resources, and the restoration of relationships as a result of their efforts to reform what was amiss. Imagine for a moment that all of this goodness, both current and conceivable, is connected to and manifested in play.

52

We need an expanded vision of community health, and in my estimation, the key is play. After almost three decades working directly and indirectly on child well-being, the adage still rings true—that you can measure the health of a community by the health of its children which often manifests itself in playfulness. Zechariah gives us an easily observed outcome of well-being that is as meaningful as many of the metrics currently used to measure community health. It is a tangible vision of the flourishing of our neighborhoods, towns, and cities and the state of countries. Whatever community we find ourselves in, whether it is a town, hollow, neighborhood, village, or city, these words speak to us because our children are centered and being engaged in one significant and very important way we can be meaningfully changed: playfully.

While the dividing line between an urban and rural context is not black and white, there are important distinctions that inform the use of "city" in scripture. We must consider biblical passages that point to the "city set on a hill" (Matthew 5:14), "cities of refuge" (Number 35:6) or "the city of God" (Psalm

48:1–3, Hebrews 11:10, and Revelation 21:2). There is a reason that cities are emphasized in casting a vision of our ultimate home and heavenly community. This is best illustrated in Hebrews 11:16. It references a city that God has prepared for His people who long for a heavenly country. We see this repeated in Revelation 21:2 as the Holy City comes down from heaven.

What did cities represent in scripture? It requires a theological and sociological consideration. Cities were fortified, and therefore, secure for the emergence of human community. Cities had infrastructure, governance, and relational systems of support that enable social systems. Cities were centers of culture and human civilization. They offered more than a common territory of shared land; they facilitated and required a shared way of life. The city, therefore, reflects a vision of how human community could develop in a shared way of life. This does not mean that rural life is somehow less than. (In most ways, what we call rural today has all the elements of biblical city life.) What must be recognized is the biblical leaning toward our shared existence in connected communities bound together with the common goal of human flourishing in deep relationship and alignment with God.

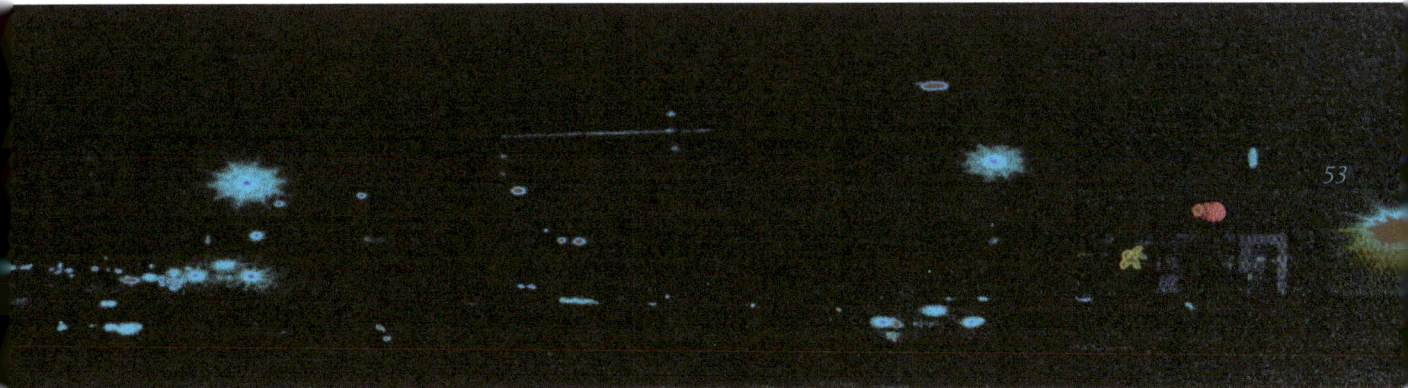

We live in an era that is characterized by two extremes in our use of language that combat and work against any sense of playfulness: volatility and sensitivity. Our language has become volatile because of how quickly and unpredictably the understanding of the words we use can change in different contexts. The word "woke" has become a great example. In one environment, it hearkens a generation back to the civil rights movement and America's awakening to the human dignity and equality of all people. In another environment, it has become a proxy word in the ongoing identity politics between left and right pundits. "Charged language" has multiplied and intensified in recent years. It leaves the average person concerned about the language they use for fear of being misunderstood. This leads to a hyper-sensitivity and in many cases, constraint of language that can speak the truth (often to power) we so badly need and that Jesus himself indicates will "set us free" (John 8:32). This effort, to use carefully chosen and acceptable words, while often well intended, can have the net effect of diminishing our responsibility to be in conversations about tough issues.

Everything from family dinners to social gatherings have become more intense, charged and animated by these two extremes. Everyone feels less safe and secure. This volatility and sensitivity constrain our language and willingness to embrace the ambiguous or metaphorical. This is dangerous because it attacks the very mechanism that has historically been essential to Christian formation, community formation, and organizational development: our imagination.

Vision — essential in any effort for transformation — is the ability to think about and/or plan for the future with imagination and wisdom. Scripture tells us in Proverbs 29 that without a vision, the people perish. We are in desperate need of visionaries and dreamers who are inspired by God or some other noble ideal to give us new ways of seeing and imagining our communities and the issues and opportunities that face them. More practically, our ability to search for truth and meaning through exploration is dependent on our ability to have open conversations that engage our imagination. And, in some cases, demand the use of our imagination in a way that allows us to lean into and "seek to understand" versus rush to judgement. We need metaphors like "city as playground" to lift our gaze and stir our imagination. A play-filled, intergenerational, city is one that begins to open my imagination to a community where enemies can become friends, issues aren't more important than the people they impact, and equity and justice for all is the norm rather than the exception for the few.

54

Play does not fill the streets of unsafe communities, and the prospect of generations of children reaching a "ripe old age" in fragile and dangerous communities is all too rare. Play happens when there is a vision for community to be a place where the cultural, social, religious, and physical systems, institutions, and structures work together to protect, provide, and produce safe havens that create the seedbed of belonging. The natural overflow of this is places and spaces where we are free to be curious, to explore, and to seek the truth together.

The book of Nehemiah gives us a vivid demonstration of the power of creating safety through a holistic vision of seeing all the systems of community development that touches the environment from physical infrastructure to cultural and religious practice. This restoration was motivated by more than the physical restoration of the walls of Jerusalem. In fact, this 52-day project to rebuild the walls came after a roughly 150-year period of ruin. The physical infrastructure was a foundation upon which Nehemiah worked to restore and strengthen the community. As we work in our own communities, the imagery of seeing the city as a playground gives us a vision of what we are working towards over the course of our lives.

Zechariah reminds us with his powerful imagery that the playing children become adults of ripe old age. We typically think of play in its most lighthearted sense. However, play has a significant developmental impact. Sadly, we have seen drastic reductions in how much children play over time. Studies, like those done by The Genius of Play, estimate that 75 percent of children below the age of 12 don't get enough play with lack of time being cited as one of the primary challenges. Some of us are living with play deficits which, in turn, produces a

lack of a "playful mindset." Play builds social skills and motivates creativity. We tend to play when we feel safe, when we are not in want, and when we are curious. Play invites us to explore new things, engage with new people, and take calculated risks. While our methods and modes change, play has benefits for us even in adulthood. We might ask ourselves what it means to cultivate a playful mindset as part of our overall competencies, and what value might we find in embracing playful environments at the appropriate time?

As we make this embrace, we must be careful to distinguish a playful environment from a competitive one. Whereas competition can happen in a playful environment, play is not always happening in a competitive environment. If we embrace the idea of our communities being playgrounds, we need to stay ever vigilant as to how and in what ways competition might rise and corrosively destroy our commitment to play. As we create more playful environments for our children and become more playful as adults, we want to make sure that this does not become some trojan horse for aggression, ambition, and antagonism. Instead, we can become more playful in ways that will create safety for the exploration of ideas,

the expansion of our conversations (participants and topics), and finding more creative solutions to our intractable challenges. This might allow us to hold our deep convictions about the power of relationships, where all are lifted up, none are diminished, and transformations that lead to human flourishing are possible.

As I close there is another outcome to Zechariah's vision of the city as a playground: the elderly with their cane in hand. One has to wonder what is capturing the attention of the men and women of ripe old age as they are sitting in the streets watching the children? I imagine they are captivated by their community and also by the play-filled streets that had previously been places of trepidation and terror. I imagine that the children physically playing deeply connects to their own playful hearts. Zechariah is hinting at something Jesus tells us more directly and forcefully in Matthew 18:1–5 that "unless you change and become like little children, you will never enter the kingdom of heaven." Seeing the city as a playground allows for a "lived reality" for children and a "relived memory" for the elderly where all—the child and the child-like—can flourish. ⊕

Dr. Dave Hillis

Aaron Dorfman

Founder and Executive
Director of A More
Perfect Union: The Jewish
Partnership For Democracy

IN CONVERSATION

DAVE: As we think about seeing the city as a playground, one of the places that we theologically pivot from is the Old Testament prophet Zechariah. Jerusalem at that point was pretty beat up and Zechariah 8 says, "Once again men and women of ripe old age will sit in the streets of Jerusalem, each of them with cane in hand because of their age. The city streets will be filled with boys and girls playing there." Zechariah was prescient in the sense that he knew that the two most vulnerable populations in any city are always the very young and the very old. So, if they are in good shape, that means that that city is actually behaving the way it's supposed to. As a result of this and many other texts, it is clear that the city is important to God. However, in some Christian circles, we have gotten away from that. There's been, whether we are conscious of it or not, an anti-urban bias.

57

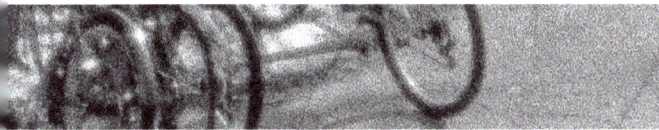

AARON: Yes, I love the provocation of this idea of characterizing the city as playground or having that as an aspirational goal. That's not a metaphor that had occurred to me before either personally or certainly in Jewish contexts. I would say that the Jewish community does not have the same negative associations with the urban that show up in in Christianity. One reason is that we have extensive texts that offer guidance about how to structure a city and the kinds of mutual obligations and responsibilities that urban neighbors have to one another.

D: What are some examples of that guidance that the rabbis gave?

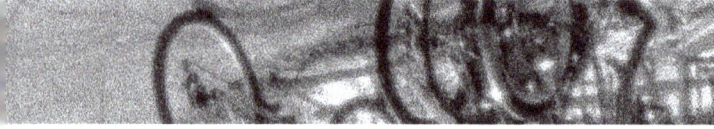

A: Much of it was very pragmatic. They talked about the need for a just city. You know, these are the kinds of things that you need in order to have a community that will be holy and that will enable its members to fulfill their responsibilities to one another—you need to have a cemetery, you need to have a central authority that allows for the disbursement of charity to the poor and the vulnerable, a place where people can study, a synagogue. All oriented around holy, social work. Part of that comes out of a rabbinic orientation toward community and the need for communities to be somewhat dense to meet the spiritual needs of their members. There's this concept that guides our sense of prayer. Fully expressive prayer can only happen when a group of at least 10 people are together. Relatedly, Jews are prohibited from traveling long distances or carrying things on Shabbat. So in order to participate in fully expressive prayer on Shabbat, you had to be close enough to your neighbors, and that was hard to do if you're living in rural areas that are really spread out.

D: Does part of that pragmatism come from the fact that for the next couple of thousand years, you are probably going to be the minority in any given space? This is how we can protect ourselves?

A: For sure. There's a piece of solidarity, capacity for mutual defense, things like that. And for much of Jewish life in Europe, Jews were prohibited from owning land, so agriculture wasn't an available economic option for them. Many of them found themselves in the trades. They were also exempt from some of the prohibitions on usury so they could serve as money lenders. They were merchants. And those are obviously occupations that lend themselves to, and can thrive in, cities in a way that they can't in rural areas.

D: I want to ask about living in negotiated spaces or in times like today where there are many perspectives and ways of seeing the world, and they seem to be running onto each other. One of the gifts of the Jewish tradition is that it facilitates different ways of seeing where all perspectives are valued, rather than a static ideology, pushing us to consider a multiplicity of voices. I'm interested in the role that metaphor plays within Judaism that allows for this diversity of perspectives and opinions. Is it explicit? Assumed?

A: I'm not a theologian or a rabbi, but metaphor is rife in biblical literature. That ethos gets expressed in the Talmud, which is divided stylistically into legal discourse and what's called aggadic discourse, which consists of stories and myths that illustrate and bring the laws to life. That's a central feature of Talmudic literature; it's used to bring life to abstract, legalistic concepts by creating fables to illustrate them. Sometimes in ways that elucidate it and sometimes in ways that complicate and almost invite interpretation that cannot be resolved definitively. So, you just keep coming back to it to consider it in new ways. When we are at our best, we're able to appreciate all of these different perspectives, though every community has its people who hold too tightly to what they think is true.

59

D: As we explore the city as playground metaphor, we've been very conscious of the fact that it could read a little naïve, pollyanna-ish. To drill further into the metaphor though, anyone who has ever been on a playground knows that there is the reality of bullies who may show up and make life very hard on the swing set or in the sandbox. We think it is possible to use the metaphor in a way that creates a vision, hope, a kind of altruism, without ignoring some of the harsher realities of life that we have got to pay attention to. Does it do both for you?

A: Yes, I think that actually helps quite a bit. The playground is very often the first venue in which a child experiences the formulation of an implicit social contract, the first relatively unmediated venue in which that negotiation takes place. That takes work. It's work to figure out how to share. To make that piece of the difficult parts of the playground explicit in the metaphor, I think, adds a layer of complexity and nuance that makes it a more useful metaphor.

60

D: With that said, how does the metaphor sit with you as you think about the Jewish experience?

A: I was just on the phone with my colleagues earlier today, having this conversation. The interesting dilemma is that we're torn between emphasizing the Jewish historical experience of persecution, the battleground story, and invoking a kind of miracle of what we as a Jewish community have built here in America. When else in human history have a whole bunch of people — a small number of whom have lived here for a really long time, meaning Native Americans — but then a whole bunch of other people from dozens or hundreds of different religious traditions, scores of different countries, different languages, some to escape persecution, some to seek opportunity, some against their will, all shown up in a place and tried to create a coherent society? And we — the Jewish community — have been able to be at the table. Given our history, that's not an opportunity we can take for granted. But we also need to be attentive to the battleground memory. We've seen the battleground and we see what has happened and we need to be very vigilant to that reality as well.

D: Absolutely. What would you say are the characteristics that need to be present at that table that you mention, for people of different faiths and different backgrounds to come together to create a playground atmosphere where there is creativity, innovation, where everyone is included?

A: I think one of the deep pathologies of this moment of intense toxic polarization is that the spaces in which we can be playful with one another feel very circumscribed. We're limited in our interactions. When we do come together, we all need a sense of psychological safety and a sense of physical safety. To stick with the playground metaphor, there has to be some way to manage the bully. And we need to feel like the stakes are not existential. Everything feels existential right now. It happens on both sides of the aisle, but at the tiniest misstep, people can just explode in outrage. I just want all of us to take a deep breath and have a little humility and a little generosity. It also is going to take principled people showing up. We're going to have to be in partnership with and collaborating with and supporting and being supported by others who are not like us. One of our strategic advisors at A More Perfect union is Dr. Hahrie Han who runs the Agora Institute at Johns Hopkins University. She says that a healthy democracy is one in which people are willing to sacrifice certainty about outcomes for certainty about process. So, if I'm going to play Capture the Flag with you on the playground, I have to be willing to lose, but I also have to know that you're not going to cheat. The rules need to be clear and fair. So, invoking those principles is important, but equally important is how we show care and concern and demonstrate real attention to each other's community by way of practice. We need to strengthen that muscle. ⊕

61

THREE.

SHALOM IN THE CITY

Rev. Dr. Terry McGonigal

Retired Director of Church Engagement and
Dean of Spiritual Life at Whitworth University

The world is changed. I feel it in the air. I feel it in the earth…Much that once was, is lost, and none now live who remember it.

— Galadriel from *Lord of the Rings*

Parker giggled with delight as she pushed the pebbles over the edge and watched them splash into the creek about 75 feet below. Suspended by two cables, the bridge stretched from spacious open fields to tall rows of corn about to be harvested. The cables were held firm by cement anchors buried into the ground, barely seen by the walkers crossing over the gulley. The most essential elements of the suspension bridge were subterranean, unseen, yet those anchors made the bridge possible, much to the joy of our granddaughter, whose laughter became ours.

Any theological conversation about shalom in the city requires a consideration of our starting point—the assumptions we make about God, ourselves, our cities, and the people who live there. Four biblical anchors—subterranean and unseen in our city's daily rhythms—provide a vision for how we get to a place where individual and communal life, economic and political life, relational and spiritual life, is renewed.

The scriptures describe with courageous honesty what has been and continues to be lost in every city each day—human dignity, economic opportunity, political justice, scarcity of basic human needs like shelter and sustenance. But this is critical: The bible also describes a way forward as we think about our cities as playgrounds instead of battlegrounds, to reach shalom in the city—"wholeness, the dynamic, vibrating health of a society that pulses with divinely directed purpose and surges with life-transforming love."[i] God's purpose and therefore our responsibility is to remember what once was lost and live in order to restore shalom in our cities.

1 Transforming Perspectives in Babylon

In the sixth century BCE, the inhabitants of Jerusalem (Israel's religious, political, and economic capital) faced an unprecedented crisis. The might of the Babylonian Empire swept down upon the city in three successive waves of destruction in the years 597, 587–586, and 582 BCE. Imagine successive attacks wiping a capital city off the map over fifteen years — that is what the Babylonians did to the city of Jerusalem as they terrorized its people with murder and destruction. Babylon was another place, like Egypt, where the Israelites were "aliens (*gerim*) in a strange land." Everything about the Babylonians was strange to the Israelites: Their geographical setting, language, food, dress, and customs. Jerusalem's inhabitants, who had now become Babylonian exiles, were overwhelmed with grief. People they once worshipped with and ate meals together with were gone. Those who survived now lived in a land not their own, among a people who brutally oppress them. How should the exiles respond?

We know that when humans are threatened we often turn to fight-or-flight responses. In an attempt to assuage their grief, the exiles envision two scenarios. First, they pray for retributive violence against the Babylonians — inflict the same kind of horror upon them that they have perpetrated upon us!

And you Babylonians — ravagers!
A reward to whoever gets back at you for all you have
        done to us;
Yes, a reward to the one who grabs your babies
And smashes them against the rocks!

— Psalm 137:8 – 9, The Message

Second, they hope for a quick resolution. Four years after the initial deportation in 597 CE, the prophet Hananiah promises the exiles that within two years God will intervene "to break the yoke of the king of Babylon." (Jeremiah 28:2 – 4, The Message). This (false) prophet promises that Judah's king along with all the exiles will return to Jerusalem with the hope of restoring the temple and worshipping their God once again. Two years — that's all!

But the prophet Jeremiah knows that in Babylonian exile neither violent vengeance nor dramatic deliverance are alternatives. Rather, what Jeremiah proposes is something far more radical. The exiles in Babylon need a transformed vision of their life in the city where they do not want to be. They need to think, act, and live differently. Jeremiah proposes a vision of radical shalom worked out over three generations in Babylon.

Build houses and make yourselves at home. Put in gardens and eat what grows in that country. Marry and have children.

Encourage your children to marry and have children so that you'll thrive in that country and not waste away. Make yourselves at home there and work for the country's well-being. Pray for the Babylonian's well-being (*shalom*). If things go well for Babylon, things will go well (*shalom*) for you.

— Jeremiah 29:5-7,
   The Message

67

Build houses, plant gardens: Take care of your basic needs while you are in exile. Think of yourselves as inhabitants of the city of Babylon. These exiles will need to learn the ways of the Babylonians—their architecture and horticulture, their culinary patterns, and economic practices. They will need to view themselves as citizens, not as gerim. The way forward depends on the exiles transforming their own understanding of who they are in this city.

Pray for the shalom of the city: This transformed perspective relies upon a prophetically shaped new understanding of God. In Jerusalem the Temple was the place where all faithful worshippers went to offer sacrifice and prayers. But the Temple has been destroyed and they are in Babylon. Does their geographical location mean that they are cut off from their God? Absolutely not! Jeremiah declares that God is present in Babylon, that God calls the exiles to pray for the Shalom of the Babylonians, for if it goes well (*shalom*) with those whom you consider your enemies, it will go well (*shalom*) with you. Jeremiah's vision could not be more counterintuitive for the Israelites at this time: Make Babylon your home. Jeremiah's shalom vision bore fruit hundreds of years later leading to shalom for another group of devastated exiles.

2 Transformed Relationships in Jericho

Narratives create impressions about cities and can impact their future. In the Bible, Jericho is one of those that gets a bad rap, but also plays an important role in several stories. Perhaps it is for that reason that at the very end of Jesus' public ministry he deliberately goes through Jericho on his way to Jerusalem for the final week of his life. By intentionally passing through this city Jesus encounters two people whose lives will be changed forever and, in turn, will change Jericho.

Entering the city, Jesus hears a man crying out, "Jesus, Son of David, have mercy on me!" His name is Bartimaeus and he is sitting by the roadside. He is an outcast being hushed by the powerful. However, the more that the crowds attempt to quiet him, the louder he cries out to Jesus, "Have mercy on me!"

Bartimaeus' appeal reaches Jesus' ears. Jesus engages him in dialogue—the antithesis of the way this crowd has responded. Bartimaeus tells his story and makes a simple request, "Lord I want to see." Bartimaeus' persistence is rewarded as Jesus acknowledges the man's trust and says, "Go ahead—see again." Now arm in arm, Messiah Jesus and Bartimaeus walk together into the middle of Jericho.

In the city another man waits for Jesus. Zacchaeus was the chief tax collector, responsible to the Romans for the extraction of taxes from the region to be paid in support of the imperial presence with its ever-present threat of violence. As the one responsible for the collection of funds in a large region, Zacchaeus had become extremely wealthy—one of the most privileged and powerful people in the whole city. Like Bartimaeus, he also wants to speak with Jesus. And, it turns out, Jesus wants to speak with him—inviting himself to the tax collector's house for a meal and a place to sleep that night. The crowds are shocked that Jesus would have anything to do with this corrupt man who has inflicted such suffering upon every resident of Jericho through his practice of unjust tax collection.

But just like with Bartimaeus, the protests of the crowd will not deter Jesus. We know nothing about the content of their conversation. But when Jesus and Zacchaeus emerge onto the street everyone recognizes that Zacchaeus is a changed man. He says it himself, "Master, I give away half my income to the poor..." Zacchaeus' confession is a recognition of his habitual extortion and the suffering he has brought upon so many. Surrounded by a multitude who have borne the brunt of his unjust collections, Zacchaeus confesses and makes restitution—all because he has met Jesus. And in that crowd stands Bartimaeus. Zacchaeus' pledge changes Bartimaeus' life. Jesus had originally restored the blind man's sight but, through Zacchaeus, now sets about restoring his social status.

I can envision the formation of a deep friendship between these two who both had encounters with Jesus. Through Jesus, they met each other. It is dynamics like this unlikeliest of friendships that give Jericho and other cities the potential to recover their reputation as cities of shalom. Indeed, this has always been the story of a city's restoration.

3

Transformed Community in Antioch

When Luke writes the book of Acts, Antioch is the third most prominent city in the Roman empire. It is the designated capital of the Roman province of Syria, which provides inhabitants cultural prominence and political power. Antioch was a crossroads for merchants to trade goods from all corners of the globe creating a truly intercultural community. There were no particularly privileged ethnic groups in Antioch because there were so many Jews and Gentiles (non-Jewish people) living together.

This is also the place where Jesus' followers are first called "Christians." The word indicates that it is a Roman term applied to those whose life reflects their commitment to Jesus and to each other. Why do they live in such strange ways, forming community and taking care of each other when they have nothing in common? There was something quite distinct about these people which merited the name Christians.

This group of people described in Acts 13 deserves analysis to understand the unique character of their community. We will consider each one in the order given in the text.

Barnabas: He first shows up two chapters earlier in Acts 11, part of the multitude dispersed from Jerusalem after the murder of Stephen. Barnabas comes from Cyprus, had spent time in Jerusalem, and now find himself in Antioch. He is sent by the Jerusalem church to Antioch to verify the report that both Jews and Gentiles were becoming followers of Jesus.

Saul: As soon as Barnabas experiences the power of the gospel at work in Antioch, he journeys to the city of Tarsus to find Saul and bring him back. Why go to all that effort? Barnabas knew that Saul, the exceptionally gifted Pharisee who was so zealous for the Jewish traditions that he became an accomplice to Stephen's murder, needed a community like the one developing in Antioch. If Saul was going to fulfill the multicultural commission laid upon him, he needed to learn how to interact with Gentiles in a manner that will draw them to Jesus. What better place to learn that lesson than at Antioch? They would immerse themselves in the fellowship of Jesus for a year.

Simeon: We don't know much about Simeon. He was probably from sub-Saharan Africa. Perhaps he was a merchant involved in the extensive practice of cross-continental trade. In Antioch Simeon encounters some Christians, and he gives himself to that community. Mentioned in this context, Simeon became an important leader for the church in Antioch representing its multicultural diversity.

'23 2 11

Lucius of Cyrene: Lucius comes from Cyrene, a city along the north African coast. At several pivotal moments in the big story of Jesus' good news, residents of the African city of Cyrene are influential in the spread of the gospel throughout the Roman empire. Lucius plays such a role here at Antioch.

Manaen: Thrice Luke includes a brief description of this man: "He had been brought up with Herod the tetrarch." What may seem like a throw away comment takes on enormous importance when we turn back just one chapter and remember that it was this same Herod who ordered the murder of James (the brother of John who wrote the fourth gospel). Whatever connections Manaen carried forward from his past, his first and primary loyalty now lies with the Christian community in Antioch and not the murderous Herod.

Saul's immersion in this multicultural Christian community sets him apart for Gentile ministry throughout the Roman empire. Manaen, Simeon and Lucius prayed for Barnabas and Saul and sent them off to proclaim the good news. This prayer service is the turning point in the book of Acts. From his experience in Antioch, Saul becomes the chief proponent of the gospel for all people, a view antithetical to his previous loyalty as a Jewish Pharisee committed to murdering Christians. The inclusion of Simeon and Lucius in this story is "a significant reminder of the barrier-breaking and inclusive nature of the gospel." [ii] God's Spirit formed a community which reflected Jesus' core values of welcoming hospitality without regard to ethnicity, gender, or class. [iii] The church at Antioch "was an international church in its own right, and it is no wonder that God chose to send missionaries to the ends of the earth from it." [iv] In the end, transformed communities transform cities.

4 Transformed City at Ephesus

After the commissioning at Antioch, Saul (now renamed Paul), travelled throughout the region visiting a variety of cities. As scholar Wayne Meeks notes, "Paul is the first urban Christian." Through his own transformative experience in Antioch, Paul was acutely aware of how Jesus' good news can change relationships in communities. Each city had its own strategic importance for the Romans, with distinct elements of religious practice, economic opportunity, and political leverage. The gospel has something to do with the unique culture of each city. Ephesus is a case study of that claim.

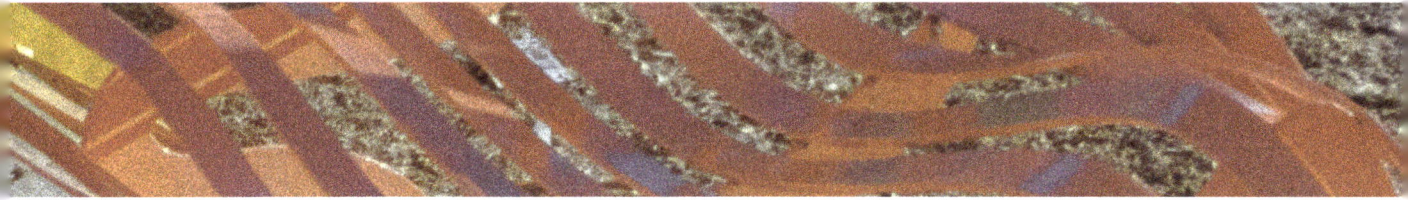

Ephesus was one of the leading cities in the Empire, exceeded only by the greatness of Rome, Alexandria, and Antioch. The city exhibits the markers of a great culture with its therapeutic baths, gymnasia, medical school, and an arena which sat over 24,000 people. At the center of Ephesian culture was the Temple of Artemis, with its 127 columns and measuring about 425 by 225 ft. The goddess Artemis was considered the source of life with her great occult powers. The temple also functioned as the central bank, collecting vast sums of money through donations made to the goddess as well as the sale of Artemis idols and occult manuals. The central focus of worship in the Artemis Temple was cultic prostitution, what today would be considered sex slavery in the name of religion.

Paul settled in Ephesus for about three years and preached the gospel in the Jewish synagogues of the city as well as in the marketplace and lecture halls to Gentiles. As in every city Paul went, over time people joined the Christian community and abandoned their religious idolatry and ceased to participate in the religiously justified corruption and exploitation rampant in the city. The power of the gospel to change lives as well as the culture of the city itself became a crisis for those invested in "the system." The Artemis idol artisans rose up and condemned Paul for threatening their religion but, more importantly, their cashflow. Under the guise of religion, they made this claim: "Not only is our little business in danger of falling apart, but the temple of our famous goddess Artemis will certainly end up a pile of rubble as her glorious reputation fades to nothing. And this is no mere local matter—the whole world worships our Artemis!" [v] Paul's life is endangered and at the insistence of his fellow believers he must flee the city immediately, never to return. Three years of relational investment in the Christian community and service in the city is swept away in one near violent afternoon.

Some six to eight years later while he was under house arrest in Rome and waiting for an audience with the Roman emperor Nero to plead his case, Paul wrote back to the Ephesians. The painful memories of his forced exile from Ephesus have been transformed into a theological reflection about humanity's relationship with God and with each other as Jews and Gentiles. As a result of God's gracious intervention in Jesus to provide a grace-filled means of salvation for both Jews and Gentiles, Paul articulates his understanding of the claim that salvation makes upon how they relate to each other. "We neither make nor save ourselves. God does both the making and the saving. He creates each of us by Christ Jesus to join him in the work he does, the good work he has gotten ready for us to do, work we had better be doing." [vi]

73

When we ask, what is this work that God has for us to do? Paul responds with one word, the same term we saw as the centerpiece of Jeremiah's exhortation to the Babylonian exiles—Shalom. Peace. Four times in the next 12 verses Paul will use the word peace. The most intense accumulation of the term we find anywhere in the Bible. Paul wants these Ephesian Christians to remember vividly all the hostility they experienced in the city and all they felt for each other as ethnic/religious Jews and Gentiles. That Jesus has intervened to transform perspectives, relationships, and even cities. This is what Paul writes in Ephesians 2:11–22:

"Jesus is our peace/shalom, who has made the two (Jew and Gentile) into one and has destroyed the barrier, the dividing wall of hostility." (v. 14)

"Jesus' purpose was to create in himself one new humanity out of the two (Jew and Gentile), thus creating peace/shalom...to reconcile both of them to God through the cross, through which he put to death their hostility (with each other)." (15–16)

"Jesus came and preached peace/ shalom to you who were far away (Gentiles) and peace/shalom to those were near (Jews). For through Jesus, we both (Gentiles and Jews) have access to the same God the Father through one Spirit." (v. 18–19)

The consequences of Jesus' work of shalom reconciles Gentiles and Jews to God and to each other. Paul wants them to live as God's fellow citizens in new Jesus-created community. To live in a such way that all the naysayers, doubters, and power-brokers in Ephesus will know that these people are followers of Jesus. The battleground of the Ephesian arena has been transformed into a new kind of temple, a building not made with human hands. Ephesus will become a new kind of city, "a dwelling in which God lives in the Spirit"—a playground where the shalom-making work of God in and through Jesus is on full display for all to see.

Transformed perspectives, relationships, communities, and cities—these are the anchors of God's shalom work in the fractured world we inhabit. Through God's Spirit and the ministry of Jesus, broken cities like Babylon, Jericho, Antioch, and Ephesus were changed into habitations where shalom took root. Over time, this produced the fruit of genuine, caring, life-giving communities. May this same transforming work take root in our cities as we work together for their shalom. "In their shalom you will find your shalom!" ◯

i Eugene Peterson, Run With the Horses, p. 148
ii Demetrius K. Williams, True to Our Native Land: An African American New Testament Commentary, pp. 232–233.
iii Galatians 3:28
iv Paul Mumo Kisau, Africa Bible Commentary, p. 1323
v Acts 19:27
vi Ephesians 2:9–10

THE WINDOW SEAT

Rev. Dr. Noel Castellanos

President of the Camino Alliance, Former CEO of the Christian Community Development Association

Recently, I was flying through Panama City on my way to Colombia. On this particular flight I was sitting in a window seat on a clear day, which gave me an amazing view of the city. As my plane descended, the sight of the city's oceanfront condos and hotels, and the multitude of magnificent high rises reaching into the heavens filled me with awe. Like most world-class cities around the world, Panama City possesses unimaginable wealth alongside extreme poverty, with millions of its residents struggling daily to survive. Sitting at the window instead of my preferred aisle seat changed my perspective.

Everyone has a different opinion regarding what needs to be done to address the challenges that exist in urban centers throughout our world: Better government, a more capitalist financial system, stronger democracy, spiritual revival, education reform, poverty reduction, more church plants, new political parties. And on and on.

Most of us are overwhelmed with the complexity of addressing the needs of our cities in a comprehensive and effective manner.

Gentrified cities are often referred to as playgrounds for the rich and famous. For ultra-rich nationals, tourists and expats, every pleasure and luxury item that a person can imagine is only a swipe away. The lure of urban life is the accessibility to consume beyond our wildest dreams, lifestyle, theater, culture, gastronomical wonders and exotic spirits of every kind. On the Panama Tourism website, read how they describe a country known to most for the Panama Canal: "A diverse multicultural city of almost 1.3 million, Panama City offers a lot more than an up-close view of the Canal. Shantytowns slink up alongside shiny high-rise condos. The Old City is an atmospheric labyrinth of churches, plazas, and

Now I have caught a glimpse of the city, my life, my faith, and my vocation from a window seat.

palaces. Fifteen miles from downtown Panama City, Soberania National Park is an excellent destination for hiking and birding. For a fascinating look at the canal, take a taxi or local bus to Miraflores Locks Visitor Center and look down on the traffic below."

The recognition of the existence of 'shantytowns slinked up alongside shiny condos' is a good invitation for considering the possibility of transforming urban battlegrounds and shantytowns into a different kind of playground.

What if what our children lack, and what our neighbors long for, is more spaces where our children can run, and jump and play both literally and metaphorically? Maybe what we need is to create more playgrounds where our children can play together, and where grandparents can shower them with love. Places where men, women and especially children have endless opportunities to run, jump, and play and no one is on the margins. Places overflowing with love, dignity and joyful exuberance — Kingdom playgrounds not only slinked up alongside shiny condos, but sprouting up on rooftops, in empty lots, in brown fields and gang-controlled battlegrounds once inaccessible to the children of the city.

This is where it gets personal for me — I became a grandfather one year ago to a beautiful granddaughter! After 40 years of working to help Latino barrios in the USA become places filled with esperanza (hope) and flowing with God's love and shalom, she has given me new perspective, energy, and motivation for continuing this calling in Latin America. The best way I can describe my change in perspective is that for many decades I have been flying seated in my preferred aisle seat on crowded planes.

And the view is magnificent!

On the day my granddaughter was born — January 4th, 2022 — I admittedly became that grandparent that can be a bit noxious to be around and I have a million photographs to prove it. She captured my heart the moment I saw her. A few months ago, one of my family members took a photograph of me with my hands extended and my facial expression filled with joy and anticipation as I awaited taking my granddaughter into my arms for a huge bear-hug. It's one of the most treasured images I possess.

Having seen, enjoyed and analyzed this photo so many times over the last few months, it has become an image that has magnified my view of how God longs to extend His arms to embrace and love all His children — including all the cities, barrios, slums, and shantytowns where the majority of the world's children live.

I am no novice to the biblical concept of God as Abba, father, or God's unconditional love likened to a mother hen tending to her chicks. Of a forgiving father running to be reunited with his prodigal son with a passionate embrace, or of Jesus' compassionate weeping for an entire city filled with suffering men, women, and children.

To these powerful images, I add the love of a doting grandfather unable to control his joy for his granddaughter.

78

On a recent trip to California with my wife, daughter, and granddaughter to visit the great-grandparents, I took Xiomara on a walk in her super cool stroller around the neighborhood. We ended up at a playground-wonderland equipped with swings, slides, and sawdust everywhere. We had a blast exploring everything it had to offer. Xiomara was probably a bit too young for the swing, but I could not control myself and had to let her experience her first swing ride with the wind blowing in her face. I'm not sure who had more fun that day, her or me!

The image of God with a crazy expression on his face as he gazes on our child-filled cities might seem unattractive or sacrilegious to many people of respectable faith, but it could infuse much need imagination and passion to the way we live out our calling to create cities and communities where everyone can thrive.

The metaphor of city as a playground will require a radical paradigm shift for most middle-class, educated, and/or wealthy Westerners. Instead of seeing world-class urban centers from the aisle, where our primary goal is to seek our own enjoyment, we need to move to the window and change our view — seeing cities through the eyes of children and adolescents living in the margins of society, longing for the love of a grandfather and a different kind of playground. I imagine this as a Kingdom playground where laughter, frivolity, safety and friendship exist without fear of rejection or exclusion. A place where class, gender, social status, or compliance to rigid religiosity are left on the sidelines and replaced by grace, empathy, and kindness. In a word, joy.

If the church is to be a significant player in this venture, we as leaders will need to design new and fresh theological frameworks that reject depictions of an angry God looking for whom to devour and replace that image with visions of a love-struck grandfather wooing their grandchildren to jump into their arms to be smothered with hugs and kisses as they hurry to the playground. This will require us to move from the comfort of the aisle to the cumbersomeness of the window.

Ten years ago, I traveled to Rio de Janeiro, Brazil with Dr. John Perkins to attend a conference on the discrimination that Black-skinned youth in the urban slums experience, resulting in the murder of multitudes of young men by local police. Exploring how the church could intervene and respond was a challenging experience. It became clear the church needed to be more present and incarnated in the shantytowns where these young men lived and struggled. Offering friendship, love and relationship was fundamental to any effort to bring about change to the suffering and injustice these children and youth were experiencing. It was such a basic realization, but so profound in its implications for deeper impact.

We also visited the world-renowned Christ the Redeemer statue at the peak of Mt. Corcovado reaching 2,300 feet into the heavens above. The statue of Christ with his arms outstretched is 98 feet high and 92 feet wide. It has become the icon of all Brazil and recognized across the world. Its original design was a large Christ with a globe in one hand and a cross in the other. Thankfully, the organizers opted to change their original design. Instead of a Christ limited to the earth and a particular theology — to extend the metaphor, an aisle seat — we have one that shows a boundless embrace that knows no limit and says 'yes' to us as individuals and our cities — a window seat. I love this image because it can help us to understand God's love for us and our cities the same way I described the photograph of me anticipating a hug with my Xiomara!

For fragile cities to experience healing and transformation, the residents of these cities must know that they are loved. They must know that Christ is present, and eagerly longing to embrace them and their cities just as surely as the statue of Christ the Redeemer is covering Rio de Janeiro with outstretched arms.

May we be motivated and empowered to extend ourselves and demonstrate lavish love to every human being created in the image of God in cities across the globe. This will transform the lives of people. This will transform our cities with Kingdom playgrounds filled with children running, jumping, playing — knowing they are loved. ⚾

PLAYING AMONG THE SYSTEMS OF THE CITY

Dr. H. Spees
Former director of Housing and Homelessness Services,
Fresno, CA, Principal, City Learners

Nelson Mandela became President of South Africa on May 10, 1994, and immediately embraced his country's nearly all white rugby team, the Springboks. The team went on to win the Rugby World Cup on June 24, 1995. Although his public display of solidarity with the team didn't solve all the ills created by the long history of apartheid, many saw Mandela's embrace of the team as accelerating national healing.

Leaders working to transform their cities share some of the same challenges as Mandela. Cities in this third decade of the 21st Century face political polarization, deaths of unarmed people of color by police, terror attacks, and mass shootings, alongside trends toward economic disparity, [i] religious hostility, [ii] and mistrust in institutions, especially religious and police institutions. [iii] In a word, battlegrounds.

81

THE KEY TO TRANSFORMING CITIES IS, LIKE MANDELA, HAVING A NEW PERSPECTIVE THAT IS FREE OF PAST RESTRAINTS AND RESTRICTIONS. THIS MEANS SEEING OUR CITIES AS PLAYGROUNDS.

Systems of the City

Transformational leaders see their cities as playgrounds in three ways: First they reject the clichéd descriptions of their city as a curse, and instead embrace their city as a blessing, a gift from God. Second, they assess their city's complex, multi-sector reality for how well its people and places are leveraging their potential and promise for the common good. And then, third, they jump in to play in heavy traffic — gathering with others to dream and decide how to link and align resources, where to put the the proverbial slide, swing sets, and sandboxes.

Dr. John Perkins articulates it this way,

> *Cities are a gift from God who is actively working through people to connect the resources of faith, city renewal, and incarnational work in neighborhoods in order to see cities socially and spiritually renewed.*[iv]

Transformational city leaders overcome the isolation and competition between sectors and institutions that lead to dysfunction and instead celebrate and accelerate the connection and collaboration that lead to transformation. When this becomes our culture, our city begins to become a common good playground.

Every system and structure becomes important — business, government, law enforcement, non-profits, churches, labor, media, public schools. What becomes abundantly clear is if a city is going to get better — look more like a playground — it is going to take collective effort. No matter what sector, institution, party, or organization is in the lead, it takes a diverse, multi-sector, multi-community team committed to collaborative action to make durable improvements. One example of this approach is the collective impact model researched and championed by Stanford University.[v]

The spark to this collaborative approach is what Communities In Schools Founder Bill Milliken calls the "relational router" — individuals, networks, and organizations — committed to cultivating the social capital required to develop the city into playground for all. A city's relational routers help a critical mass of leaders to think about meaningful and sustainable change by moving away from old patterns of self-interest, disconnection from an increasingly alienated community and competition between neighborhoods and institutions.

The Church's Role in the Systems of the City

Toward the end of his career, Peter Drucker, the renowned management consultant who shaped the understanding and function of the modern business corporation, focused his energies on the social sector. In a workshop with national church leaders he said, "The Church is the only institution capable of re-civilizing broken urban environments." He went on to clarify, however, that "the church is the most fragmented institution in any city." Drucker believed that each one of the structures, institutions and neighborhoods that make up the city are generously populated with people of faith. He challenged the church to recruit, develop and distribute faith-filled leaders as relational routers for the common good, operationalizing their faith in their context, for the flourishing of their entire city.

A Church that nurtures these relational routers becomes salt and light, perhaps even the "city on a hill" portrayed by Jesus in Matthew's gospel. The Church is at its best when its people permeate the systems and structures of a city with a spirit of sacrificial service that leads to the joy of seeing people and places transformed.

A City of Shalom

In planning, we often talk about 'beginning with the end in mind.' In the case of cities, the end is *shalom*: the recognition that the concept of city is a *gift* that flows from a theology of God's providential common grace for all. *vi* God created cities so that humans might flourish.

When peace is defined only as an individual, internal spiritual experience, we fail to understand it as the goal of city transformation. As an example, in the Church we've discovered that peace in race relations is *not* when tearful—even sincere—white men ask forgiveness of Black men in a conference setting and then go back to business as usual without any ongoing relational or social justice outcomes. Peace requires long-term relationships forged between pastors, community activists, residents, and law enforcement officials across racial, cultural, and class boundaries in ways that provide a foundation for regular access, communication, accountability, transparency, and trust.

Real peace is the difference between the quiet of martial law after a riot versus the deep—and imperfect—peace forged through the Truth and Reconciliation Commission hearings, a court-like process that restrained violence by restoring a level of trust and justice after the abolition of South African apartheid in 1994. *vii* Mandela was crucial in ensuring it took place.

Working for peace in cities involves risk, like convening a summit of gang leaders to discuss a cease fire, or like leading a church full of Polish workers in Gdansk, Poland to declare solidarity against Communist repression.*viii* Or like respectfully redirecting a group of Black Lives Matter marchers attempting to shut down a state highway as D.J. Criner, an African American pastor, did in 2015 here in my city of Fresno, California, heading off a confrontation between 300 protestors and 20 highway patrol officers in full riot gear.

But as complicated and risky as it can sometimes be, working for peace can also be simple—as simple as the Old Testament picture of old folks sitting on their porches while children play in the street (Zechariah 8:4). As we say at Leadership Foundations: a playground.

83

But this simple picture of a playground implies a community engaged in a complex set of actions. To see kids and seniors delight together in the safe streets of their city requires an urban environment where all of the systems and structures of the city are working together; where leaders and the resources they steward in education, business, law enforcement, government, faith communities, and health care are all pulling in the same direction for the benefit of all the people of the city, especially for the most vulnerable and those at the margins.

Cities as God's playground is when everything works for everybody all the time, and no one is left out. Peace is God's goal for our cities. And when peace is achieved—even partially—there is joy.

This vision of systemic and structural peace makes people and families and neighborhoods whole. The Biblical concept of shalom, the Hebrew word for peace, fortifies this vision because shalom means the experience of wholeness, a comprehensive, positive relationship between God and humans and between humans and each other, spiritually, economically, politically, socially, including the institutions, organizations, congregations, and communities that shape their lives.

Peace works as a goal for cities when defined in a way that instills hope while still facing and addressing their harshest urban realities. Peace based on the Bible's definition of shalom stands strongly against injustice and oppression, confronts and changes unjust systems and structures, stands with victims against oppressors, and ultimately seeks to transform society.[ix]

Working for peace in cities—making them more like playgrounds—means playing in the heavy traffic of complicated and diverse urban environments. Like rugby, there are scrums, tackles, rucks, mauls, and sometimes blood, sweat, and tears. It demands understanding the interplay among sectors, institutions, and communities and the complex differences that fuel conflict. It calls for building collaboration between competing organizations, connecting, allocating, and utilizing a wide variety of scarce resources in ways that achieve measurable, sustainable quality-of-life results in lives and neighborhoods, fairly and equitably.

From Mother Teresa living among the dying in Calcutta; to Dr. Henley Morgan, a businessman who moved his family and businesses into the Trenchtown area of Kingston, Jamaica, now employing over 150 residents; to John and Vera Mae Perkins, leaving a middle class life in California to return to live in a segregated and violent Mississippi in the 1960's, becoming grandparents to a movement of women and men relocating their homes and churches into under-resourced communities around the world; to Father Greg Boyle's Homeboy Industries planted in downtown Los Angeles, offering opportunity and a way out to hundreds trapped in gangs; to Jember Teffera, the wife of the former Mayor of

84

Addis Ababa, and her comprehensive development of multiple neighborhoods in Ethiopia's capital city through education, health care, housing, infrastructure and business development; to Bob Lupton, developing strategies of reinvesting in disinvested neighborhoods in Atlanta; the past 50 years have seen hundreds of multi-generational, multi-cultural, multi-sector Christ-followers moving into, staying put in, or returning to tough urban environments with their homes, churches, ministries and businesses. And these expressions of the Incarnation have changed individual lives, families, neighborhoods, and institutions in cities around the world. And personally, I have witnessed this type of gritty, Christ-following, strategic work being lived out in my city of Fresno for over 30 years. Today, 22 neighborhoods identified by the Brookings Institute for their "concentrated poverty" have become strategic focal points for investment by congregations, students, social enterprises, and the city government itself. We are seeing both macro and microcosms of playgrounds erupting in the urban landscape of our world.

In reflecting on the Springboks' victory, Mandela declared,

> *Sport has the power to change the world. It has the power to inspire. It has the power to unite people in a way that little else does. It speaks to youth in a language they understand. Sport can create hope where once there was only despair. It is more powerful than governments in breaking down racial barriers. It laughs in the face of all types of discrimination.*[x]

Mandela's intuition of the power of play works for those of us involved in the tough sport of transforming our cities. Serious, risk-taking, peace-seeking play promises joy to those seeing their cities as God's playgrounds. ⊗

i http://www.cbpp.org/research/poverty-and-inequality/a-guide-to-statistics-on-historical-trends-in-income-inequality

ii http://www.pewforum.org/2014/01/14/religious-hostilities-reach-six-year-high/

iii http://www.gallup.com/poll/183593/confidence-institutions-below-historical-norms.aspx *Confidence in US Institutions Still Below Historical Norms; Confidence in religion, police at all-time lows*

iv *Dr. David C. Hillis,* Cities: Playgrounds or Battlegrounds — Leadership Foundations' Fifty Year Journey of Social and Spiritual Renewal, *p 2. Dr. John Perkins is founder of Christian Community Development Association (See www.ccda.org)*

v https://clearimpact.com/wp-content/uploads/2016/10/The-Components-of-Effective-Collective-Impact.pdf *accessed 2-2-23*

vi *Robert Benedetto and Donald K. McKim,* Historical Dictionary of the Reformed Churches, *2nd ed. (Lanham, MD: Scarecrow Press, Inc., 2010), 195. God's grace — his overall, generous provision to all of humanity — is unconditional blessing extended by God for: 1.) the maintenance of life (common grace) and for 2.) the purpose of salvation and perseverance in the Christian faith (special grace).*

vii http://www.cbpp.org/research/poverty-and-inequality/a-guide-to-statistics-on-historical-trends-in-income-inequality

viii https://thevieweast.wordpress.com/2015/07/29/the-evolution-of-the-polish-solidarity-movement/ *(accessed July 21, 2016)*

ix *Perry B. Yoder,* Shalom: The Bible's Word for Salvation, Justice, and Peace *(Nappanee, IN: Evangel Publishing House, 1987), 5. "Shalom, biblical peace, is squarely against injustice and oppression...Shalom demands a transforming of unjust social and economic orders. Rather than being a message addressed to victims, shalom acts against oppressors for the sake of victims. In the Bible, shalom is a vision of what ought to be and a call to transform society."*

x https://www.globalgoals.org/news/sport-for-development-and-peace/ *Accessed 2-1-23*

WHOSE

PLAYGROUND?

Father James Alison
Author, Priest and Public Theologian

Playgrounds are terrifying places for some of us, and cities places of relief. Some of us get socialized into the former by becoming locked into a mode of hypervigilant survival. While over time the latter offer us chances of working our way out of that, re-socializing ourselves through new interactions.

While we were dragooned by teachers in classes, all was well: there was structure and order. But when the bell rang and we went to the playground, oh the terror! Governed entirely by peer tyranny. With adults taking up their stations at distant outposts, guarding against only the most egregious violence — none of them on the inside of our waves of desire, learning, fantasy, loves, hates, and fears. None able to speak a word into our hearts from our level.

Who's in, who's out? Who's cool, who's not? Who has famous relatives, who doesn't? Who's, well, different? Will they have me in their gang? Whose hint of lesser or of greater being is revealed by clothing, tales of travel or lack thereof, brand-named backpack or toy? How painful is the swirling of that desire, the changing of groups, alliances, belonging. How stressful to keep up. Those who are teaching us to be good little girls or boys, not breaking rules, don't seem to appreciate that just beneath their gaze, yet, oh how far beyond it, we are run by a wild jungle; that the "other" which runs us, which we are to each other, knows nothing of rules.

The rules stand moot and looking on, until we learn to enfold them and their adult enforcers as props within our struggles.

At the same age as we are Sunday-schooled into hearing of Adam and Eve, Cain and Abel, we are Monday-schooled into hearing of Romulus and Remus and other classical myths. And even without hearing those tales, we reproduce their structure unwittingly. Yet, how rare it is that someone reassures us by telling us that our desires are not our own. That it is normal that we be run by those we run with.

Even so, that we needn't be frightened of those who make things seem desirable to us; they are only a trap if we let them be; if we don't learn to filter out where they do us good and where they do us harm. We may indeed be consumed by moments of murderous jealousy of those whom we would desire to be like; but that doesn't define us unless we let it. That to find and re-find belonging by casting out one weaker than ourselves, although hard beyond words to resist, is not "just the way things are." Except afterwards, when we need to justify it. How

88

painfully mysterious is that space of beckoning adulthood where we half know what we are doing, half know who we will become as we do those things, and half refuse that knowledge since it puts too great a crimp on our survival.

Yet the story that began with an expulsion from a garden, and a murder in a field, ends with a city. A most curious city, since it has no temple, and no light. Neither is necessary, for all present are illuminated by the Lord God and the Lamb. What does that mean? That this City is formed by those who have worked out, each one, their own way beyond playground rules. All are illuminated by the one they were inclined to throw out. All have allowed themselves to be recreated by that one, to be forgiven.

So, is our city to be the one formed by the playground that we had, where all we learnt is hardened into destiny and fate? Or are we to recover the playground that we almost had, the one that, half-glimpsed, could have been, but was not? The act of recovery, fuelled by the half glimpse become full dream and living vision, is our playground city. The playground is in the how rather than the what.

What does it look like, this act of recovery? It starts of course from some sideways glance of forgiveness which reaches us when we see as friend the class fairy, the sissy, the stinky one, the "one of 'them'" of our earlier playground. Not necessarily the same person, maybe some later avatar, occupant of an all too familiar place. One who triggers awareness of how what went before is still upon us. Then we may remember how shallow was the success of fake unity against that one, how little security it gave. We may remember who we became when we went along with, or guided, that pointing of the finger, relieved that, at least for now, it did not point at us.

And as we receive that painful memory, we lose our founding "we," and thus our identity. For forgiveness—as we are forgiven—uncovers our sameness with those over against whom we became who we are. We can tell we are being forgiven not when we feel sudden innocence for all that we have done, but when we discover ourselves held securely in affection, no longer needing to protect ourselves against our shame. This holding of us in affection gradually opens up to us the same one from whom we were fleeing, but now as gateway to fresh future.

89

When Paul tells us that God reconciling the world to Godself takes the form of us becoming ambassadors of Christ, with God appealing through us, it is to this that he refers. That we find ourselves being befriended by the stinky one, the sissy, whoever the cast out one is, the avatar of Christ, and finding that who we really are comes from them, not over against them. Once we have seen that, a new precarious "we" is already beginning to come into being. For we quickly pick up that there are a whole lot of cast-out others, bearers of oh-so-many convenient stereotypes. And that as our half-deliberate blindness is stripped away, so each of these are found to be gifts to us and who we will become.

It is at this point that we fall through the false lure of the city founded as battleground, and so to be re-founded every day. The first owner of the Daily Mail, the UK's most notorious tabloid, told its first editor: "Give them, each day, someone to hate." And as we see through that, we lose our place in the security of a world of winners and losers, of fake binaries dressed up in prestige and glory. Someone who lives as a sojourner, a resident alien, who has no abiding city, is not someone on the run. It is someone who has defected in place from the fake order of scapegoating, who has begun to detect the real along with others who have been able to lose the grip that founding terror has upon them, have been set free from its story of power and sacrifice. Because they have begun to detect and live the real, they can also discover and be discovered by sisters and brothers like themselves, those for whom finding their way into creation is an adventure, not a duty or a chore.

This is the discovery of the real playground that lives tall and breathes free beneath pomps and lures. The playground where I do not reach out as if from above to marginalised or formerly marginalised others, but where I allow myself to become precarious as I am gifted by those whose precariousness is bringing me into being as part of a new "we." For what is precariousness but the gift of being vulnerable enough to be created? To trust the adventure, resting on a power other than my own, receiving the dream of the One who makes all things new.

What is genuinely surprising about this is that it escapes from all moralism. I come to see the humanity in others, not as a determination of some ideology, a grudging deduction from something I'm supposed to know. Rather it glows through lives narrated, rich embers being blown into flames from which I had long since sought to protect myself. And as this happens, as I lose my privileged control, I notice that at first the warmth, and then the sparks, and finally the flame itself has come to rest on this brightening ember who had long despaired he'd ever have a heart.

90

And that this is not a poetic fantasy flight from the cruelty of reality. It is what is real breaking through the dull and fantastic deceptions of cruel idols. And what is real is playful, it dances, because hearts made supple enliven both stories and faces, and death takes nothing away. For as city dwellers from Augustine to Chesterton have known, and Pope Francis reminds us, God is younger than all of us. ⊗

DR. DAVE HILLIS

FATHER

JAMES

MARTIN

American Jesuit priest, writer, and
editor-at-large of *America Media*

In Conversation

Dave: We have been playing with the idea that humankind is metaphorical. For example, God is Father. People have a lot of investment in that but at the end of the day, it's a metaphor, right? And so, if that's true, and metaphors are what actually help us interpret the world around us and make meaning out of it, then it seems that the great task at hand is for us to begin to be conscious of the metaphors we are using to interpret life.

92

James: That's a wonderful insight. Yes, it's what Jesus does in all the parables, right? Last Sunday, it was, "God is like the shepherd who searches for the sheep, God is like the prodigal father." One of the great lines is from Walter Brueggemann. He said that stories open up our minds in ways that arguments cannot. And I would say that images do the same thing. An image can open up our mind. A metaphor can open up our mind in a way that an argument or a definition cannot. I usually think of these things in terms of stories, stories open up our minds, but a metaphor can do the same thing because it's very poetic, right? So, God is the Good Shepherd. People love that. I think of Pope John XXIII, who said, "The church is not a museum, it's a garden." That's something that's totally different. And Pope Francis' idea is a little obscure, but he said the church is like a field hospital. It's really powerful.

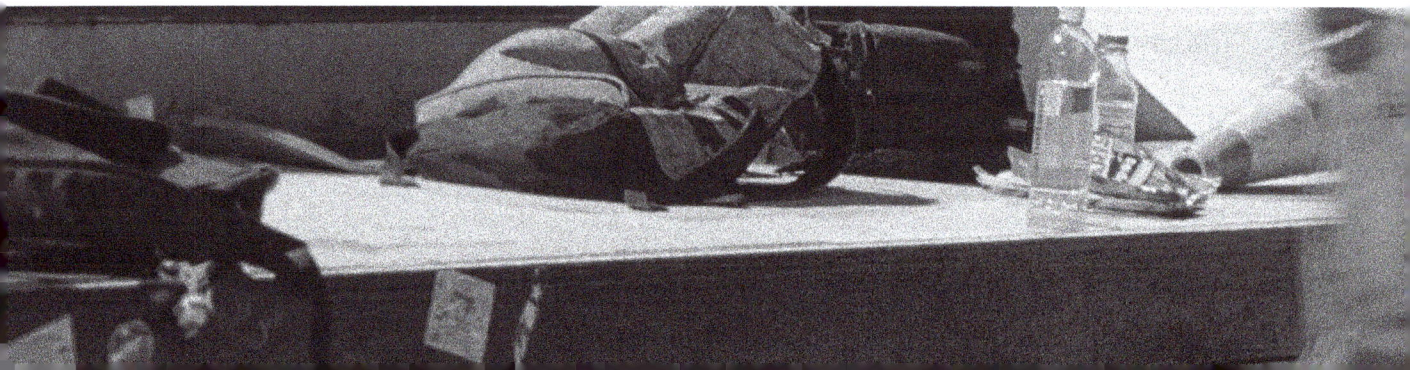

D: I've wondered then, if a lot of the collisions that are taking place in society, whether it's political or ideological, is the result of these unexamined metaphors that are shaping the way that we see, and we just run right into each other almost without knowing why we do.

J: Yes. There was a movie made about my LGBT ministry called "Building A Bridge." And they interviewed this guy who was kind of an opponent. And he said, "The church is like a sandbox, either play within the rules or get out." And I just thought that's the worst image of the church I've ever heard. But that's his image, right? If you have an image of the church as a sandbox or the church as a classroom where there's one right answer and everything else is wrong, and if I have an idea of the church as the field hospital, or the church, as a mystery, then absolutely, we will clash because you can just keep coming at me with "You're not playing by the rules" and I can keep coming at you with "You don't understand the mystery."

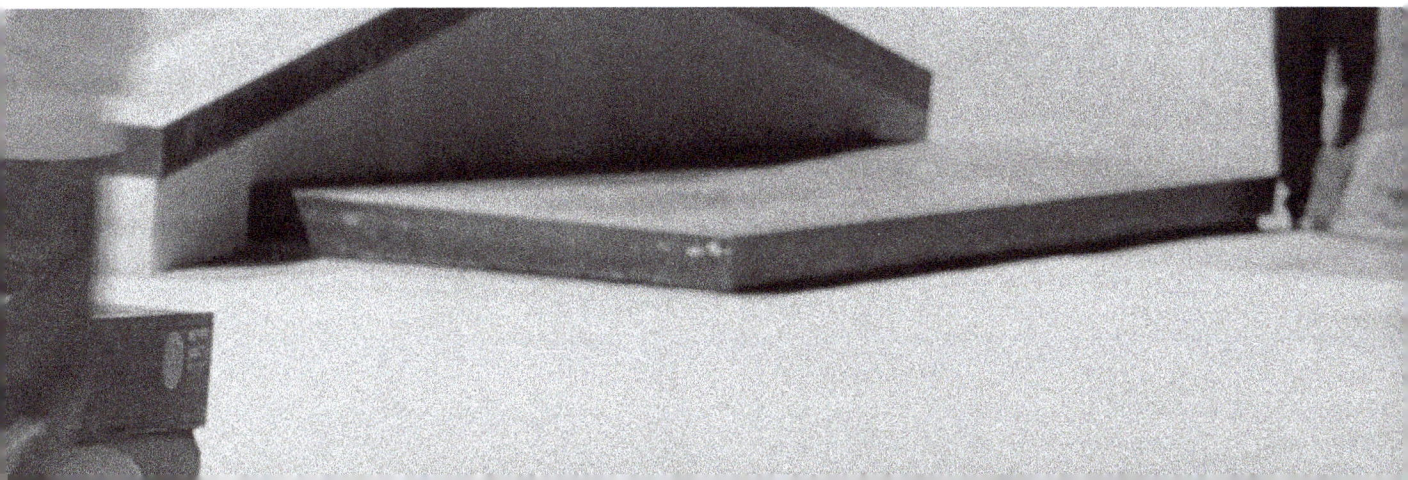

93

D: So, if we ever are to examine our metaphors that explain how we come at these different issues, how would you see that taking place?

J: I think one of the difficulties is getting people to think in that way at all. And so, if you're wedded to the metaphors the church has historically used, you can get stuck pretty quickly. For example, let's use one the church has been fond of: God as Judge. That's probably one of the most common. If that's what you've been taught your whole life, then you believe that the only way to please God is by following the rules. Any challenge to thinking about God differently than that is very difficult. I think one of the challenges is to encourage and invite people to think about new images and that's hard.

It happens in the Gospels. Jesus is constantly giving us these images and people still have a hard time with them. I think the key question is: Can you invite people in a beautiful way to see metaphor and tease out the implications for themselves? There's a line from a Jesuit I like, Carlos Valles, who says, "If you always imagine God in the same way, you will not be open to the new ways that God has in store for revealing Himself to you." And that's the key question: Are we open? Some people can't do it.

94

D: Knowing that it is hard work, what kind of tools have you developed in your toolbox?

J: I think the key to it all is the word invitation. You know: Have you ever thought about it this way? Not being prescriptive by saying, "This is the metaphor," but rather, "Hey, here's an interesting metaphor. What do you think it might mean?" I also think doing it in a charitable way is helpful.

D: Like Emily Dickenson, "Tell the truth but tell it at a slant?"

J: Exactly. And frankly the greatest tool we have in the church is relying on the person of Jesus. Jesus did the same thing. When Jesus was asked, "Who is my neighbor?" What does he do? He does not say, "Here are the 10 things that make up a neighbor." He says, "A man went down to Jericho," and tells the Parable of the Good Samaritan. It's really amazing. And then people were probably asking themselves, "What does that mean?"

D: Exactly. Like Nicodemus and the woman at the well. I would make the argument that what's at play there is a metaphor change.

J: Yes, Jesus treats these two people in very different ways and uses these metaphors to meet them where they are — one very much on the margins, and one really in the center of power. So he's going to this real powerful person, and to this woman who has to be at the well at 12 o'clock because she's been ostracized. He's using metaphors with both.

This is hard to hear, but some people just aren't open to it. They're not and that's where Jesus says, "They listen, but they don't hear." That's a hard thing. No matter how elegant and beautiful and well-crafted and inviting and accessible and non-threatening your story is, some people just won't listen.

D: You often tell stories when you are speaking or in your writing. Is there something in particular about Jesuit spirituality that is conducive to this whole world of story and metaphor?

J: Oh yeah. The Spiritual Exercises invite people to imagine themselves in Scripture scenes. And that means putting yourself in the story imaginatively. So that's the first thing. The second thing is seeing yourself and God as part of your story, right? God takes an active interest in your story. However, I come back again and again to imagining yourself in Scripture. And again, that's really hard for people who want you to tell them what to think. And you know, Jesus doesn't do that. Jesus says, "Hey, a man went down to Jericho..." and now we are off into a story with all kinds of possibilities.

D: As we examine this metaphor of seeing the city as a playground, we have been surprised at the importance of play itself. Is that something that needs to be reinstituted by us in terms of our work that at times can be dreadfully serious and very sober minded? Do we lose something if we're not playful?

J: I talk a lot in my book, "Between Heaven and Mirth," about Jesus as playful. There are so many instances of his humor that we overlook. Jesus himself was playful. The first thing I love is, he uses word play in his saying that certain religious leaders, "strain out a gnat but swallow a camel," for example. The Aramaic words are galma for gnat and gamla for camel. So it's wordplay. He calls his disciples by nicknames: "You're the rock" and "You are the sons of thunder." That's the case even with Mary Magdalene. Some scholars think that "Magdalene" means "tower." And Jesus's primary image of the kingdom is a feast, the wedding feast, the joyful banquet. His first miracle, after all, is to make more alcohol at a party. When you hear it that way, you think, "Well, yeah, he did!" I think we do have to recover all of this, and it can best be summed up in one word: Joy.

And I think this image of the city as a playground is great and helps with this task. It allows us to begin recovering that idea of God as play. And what does it mean? That doesn't mean it's not serious. I would connect it more deeply to joy. Jesus talks about that constantly: "That my joy in you might be complete," he says.

So, what does it mean to be on the playground? One of the things I like about the metaphor a lot is that it is so unexpected. The novelty and the uniqueness of it, and even the kind of challenge of it, is a good thing. Because you could say that the city should be like such and such and we would all say, "That's nice." But the benefit of the playground metaphor is that it's really new and it's unique, and I'd never heard it. And the question is, how do we tease that out? And what does it mean to be on a playground? ⚾

97

FO UR.

WHAT MAKES YOU COME ALIVE ?

Rev. Dr. Troy Jackson
Author and Co-Founder of UNDIVIDED, State Strategies Director, Faith in Action

On April 29th, 1992, an all-white jury found the police officers who beat and pummeled an unarmed Black man named Rodney King not guilty. In the coming days, South Central Los Angeles became a flashpoint of racial unrest.

I was a student at Princeton Seminary and our school president called a meeting at Miller Chapel to reflect on the verdict and subsequent violence. When I walked into the room, I quickly noticed that there were not a lot of people there who looked like me: a white guy. Most of the Black students on campus showed up. A number of Korean and Korean American students showed up (Koreatown businesses were greatly affected by the unrest in LA). But out of roughly 600 white students on campus, only about a dozen showed up.

 I stayed at the meeting, which was filled with tension, anger, and lament. As it was wrapping up, a Black student suggested that those who want to do more than talk about this should connect and plan a follow up meeting. I stuck around and said I wanted to get involved. Over the next year, I was part of Seminarians for Justice. We went to a march in Washington, D.C. and advocated to end racial profiling in stores in downtown Princeton. I began to learn how to organize for racial justice.

Looking back, fellow Black and Asian students had invited me to join a multiracial playground of innovation, creativity, connection, healing, and love as we struggled together for racial justice.

Three decades later the United States is still divided along racial and ethnic lines and marred by racial injustice. We are stymied at the national and local levels by a generational sin that breaks the heart of God and deeply wounds people created in God's image.

We feed the beast of racism when we buy into the lie that some people—some races and ethnicities—are more valuable than others. These dynamics set up the racial battleground that has shaped our public struggle for justice. Dehumanizing systems, including forced removal, slavery, reservations, internment camps, and segregation, all undergirded by racialized and often state sanctioned violence, are not the conditions necessary to foster a playground.

Yet even in the midst of horrific injustice, voices at the front lines have often been rooted in a deep faith in our common humanity. Martin Luther King, Jr., as leader of the Southern Christian Leadership Conference, centered all their work in the spirit of the organization's motto: To Redeem the Soul of America. Embedded in this profession is the conviction that all people are worthy and capable of redemption, individually and collectively.

At UNDIVIDED, our mission is to unite and ignite people for racial justice. The order is important. Discovering our shared stories and shared humanity creates the conditions to make redemptive action possible. And we are of the mind that being able to see the city as God's playground helps make these conditions real.

It's easy to surround ourselves only with people who share our beliefs and convictions about everything from faith to politics to what sports teams we follow. We can also surround ourselves with people who are like us racially, ethnically, and socio-economically. Further, where one lives has the potential to lead to an echo chamber and social media can have an exponential effect on that echo. The algorithms on Facebook, Twitter, Instagram, TikTok, and other social media spaces tailor (through microtargeting) the news we each see and the voices we hear from.

Once you find yourself in this echo chamber, you are primed to divide the world into us versus them.

You are likely to view your city as a battleground, a contested space that must be saved or protected from the other.

We call this divided battleground a place of stagnancy. Stagnant water is water that is contained and has no flow. We have a very small pond near our house (some might call it a puddle), but it is large enough that, if left to stagnate all summer, it would quickly become a breeding ground for mosquitoes, attract other pests, and become a toxic stew. To prevent this, we have a fountain we turn on every day beginning in April all the way into October to keep the water flowing.

If we are to make our cities into playgrounds instead of battlegrounds, we need a lot less stagnancy and a lot more flow. Stagnancy breeds distrust, division, greed, injustice, fear, and violence like mosquitoes that swarm and irritate our shared public life.

Our vision at UNDIVIDED is to see "a flow of racial healing and justice that repairs wounds and cultivates equitable systems where all people flourish." When imagining the difference this would make in our cities, we turn to Ezekiel 47.

102

The prophet Ezekiel was in exile in Babylon following the fall of Jerusalem and the destruction of the temple. Near the end of the book bearing his name, he has a vision of a rebuilt temple in Jerusalem. After going through the dimensions of the new temple, Ezekiel sees water flowing from the temple, down the mountain, and toward the Dead Sea. The Dead Sea has that name for a reason — it has a salt level of roughly 34%. Nothing can live in it.

But in Ezekiel's vision, the water flowing from the temple turns the Dead Sea back to life. People fish its waters, which are teeming with fish on par with the nearby Mediterranean Sea. And along the shores of the flowing water are trees that bear fruit for the nations, and leaves that offer healing. Ezekiel's vision suggests that when we get it right, the Church and followers of Jesus ought to be a fountain of life, healing, provision, and justice. Our cities should be much better places for everyone because we are there, and God's spirit is flowing through our lives.

We have found that when we bring people together across differences with vulnerability and sincerity, to share stories, reflect, and explore the impact of systemic racism, perspectives are changed.

Peer-reviewed research supports this. Dr. Hahrie Han, founding director of the SNF Agora Institute at Johns Hopkins University, and her colleague Maneesh Arora studied those who participated in our cohorts over a few years found that members make three big shifts when they take part in an UNDIVIDED cohort. First, they grow in empathy, or the ability to take the perspective of and feel alongside someone different than themselves. Second, they move from isolation to community. And finally, the move from passivity to action.

We saw this happen when we did a cohort with an all-white police department and a group of Black residents in a small township near Cincinnati. When we began facilitating our first session, UNDIVIDED co-founder Chuck Mingo and I felt like we were stepping into a battleground. A few of the officers had the thin blue line flag as a part of their Zoom background. The black residents were on edge. The officers were silent. Then the police chief demonstrated leadership by sharing vulnerably and with humility. A Black resident who helped bring the group together did the same. And soon

the group began to share stories, laugh, and see one another's humanity.

During the last week, the police chief confessed that the slogan "Black Lives Matter" had always triggered him. But having been part of the cohort, and having listened and learned from Black participants, he now recognized that for far too much of our history, and far too often even today, the message many African Americans receive is that their lives don't matter, so he committed to doing all he could to make sure that the slogan became a reality in his township and community.

Then a Black resident shared. She said that when she joined the cohort, it was primarily to set the police officers straight, and she felt she had done some of that over the six-weeks. But then she shared that when she saw police in uniform, all she saw was their profession, and viewed them as a threat. She realized she had been in her own echo chamber, unable to recognize the humanity of the person behind the badge. She committed to seeing any person in law enforcement as a human being first from that moment on.

Over those six-weeks, what started as a battleground turned into a playground. We have now had a second cohort with this police department and the community, and they are doing ongoing work to stay connected, to push for racial justice, and to make their community safe and secure for every person, and particularly for Black and Brown people in their township.

But if we are going to make our metro areas true playgrounds, we must work to make them places where all people can flourish, which demands systemic change. Far too often followers of Jesus stop short, flinching when the struggle for justice demands ongoing collective action to address systemic inequities. In Cincinnati, this looked like a two-year campaign to raise taxes $15 million every year to fund high quality preschools for our most vulnerable early learners, the majority of whom are Black and Brown children. In Illinois, it looked like a team holding educational forums, having house meetings, and going to the state capital to lobby to ensure an end of cash bail in the state

(cash bail often means that poorer people, who are disproportionately Black or Brown, must await trial in a cell rather than at home simply because of a lack of resources).

We also need to be clear: Any playground I've ever seen has tension and conflict. Children on playgrounds get their hands dirty, compete for space on the slides, seesaws, and swings, and learn to negotiate, take turns, and make room for everyone. Playgrounds are not perfect, and they are often places of struggle. But ultimately, when the playground is all that it can be, they are places of fun, joy, and adventure. They are places where every person comes alive.

One of my favorite theologians is Howard Thurman, whose book *Jesus and the Disinherited* is one of the must-read books to come out of 20th Century US Christianity. Thurman once wrote, "Don't ask what the world needs, ask what makes you come alive and go do it. Because what the world needs is for you to come alive." ⚙

THE DIRTY METAPHOR

THAT CROSS-CONTAMINATED MY SPIRITUAL IMAGINATION

Chelsea Langston Bombino
Program Officer of The Fetzer Institute

Then he showed me a river of the water of life, clear as crystal, coming from the throne of God and of the Lamb, in the middle of its street. On either side of the river was the tree of life, bearing twelve kinds of fruit, yielding its fruit every month, and the leaves of the tree were for the healing of the nations.
— Revelation 22:1–2 (cf Ezekiel 47)

We often say the story of God's creation follows the arc from garden (Eden) to city (New Jerusalem). While this is true in one sense, the narrative as this above passage in Revelation captures is more complex. The image that comes to mind for me is not a city alone, but a garden in a city, or a city in a garden. The notions interface with one another. A both/and. When we seek the playgrounds — the varied parks, gardens, and greenspaces — in our own urban centers, both our incarnated realities and our spiritual imaginations expand. The lush, biodiverse abundance of a garden cohabiting with the fecund pluralistic tapestry of a polis. The New Jerusalem where God's whole community of creation — human and more-than-human — thrive in their differences together. The floral metropolis. The aromatic civitas. The city as playground.

Etymological and Spiritual Roots of Playground

The meaning of the combined noun playground first emerged in the late 18th century. The roots of play and ground, separately, are much older. The word history of the verb play goes back at least to Old English plegan, connoting interconnected meanings: the making of music, children's merriment, frolic, engagement in sport. The Old English grund, the etymological grandmother of the modern ground, contains a variety of referents, some of them seemingly contradictory: surface layer of the Earth, deep place, bottom of the sea, abyss, Hell.

This incomplete overview of the linguistic predecessors of our modern conception of playground may at first glance complicate the task at hand — unearthing the fertility of the metaphoric meaning of cities as playgrounds. When I think of playgrounds, the first thing that comes to mind is the Kaboom! build my husband and I participated in several years ago in West Baltimore. Local families from the school, along with volunteers from a tapestry of local civil society organizations, came together for a few days to dig, plant, sort, assemble and ultimately create a safe, welcoming space for children to play at recess.

Playground. Neon dyed plastic tubes. Recycled tire floors to provide an environmentally friendly cushion for children who fall. Something that can be constructed in a few days: Kaboom!

These archetypal images of playgrounds are not wrong, in fact they offer many wonderful benefits to children, families, schools, and larger communities. This is especially true in dense urban areas where safe spaces for play and gathering are increasingly rare. But whenever we limit our metaphors to the most basic of images, we limit our capacity to unfurl the full potential of the metaphor itself, designed, at its best, to help us think beyond the confines of stereotype. Metaphors help us fall in deeper love with the places we inhabit. They are portals to more complicated and fertile understandings of place itself.

But how is love of place cultivated? Does one fall in love with a place and then decide it is a playground or is it the reverse where you first see cities as playgrounds and then begin to see their faint outlines in your city?

108

Urban Garden Cemeteries as … Playgrounds?

What were the playgrounds of cities before playgrounds even existed, in the modern sense? According to the GardenDC Podcast, one answer to this question was garden cemeteries. They were the first public gardens, the first large publicly designed urban green spaces set aside, the first city parks. Thinking of garden graveyards as playgrounds certainly expands and deepens the metaphor of city as playground, but does it take it too far? Is it too morbid? Too much?

Many botanists already see older cemeteries as playgrounds, places where, by accident or design, heirloom roses are kept alive. Two hundred years ago, local, state, and national parks did not exist, so garden cemeteries were really the first public playgrounds in many towns and cities. In centuries gone by, elaborate funerary architecture and blooming nurseries welcomed the public to play with and among their ancestors. There was integration between the land of the living and the land of the dead.

And, during the pandemic, many urban and suburban garden cemeteries have experienced a revival in the eyes of the public as a destination for recreation. More and more urbanites throughout the pandemic have sought out the cemetery as a place of play. According to Greg Tepper, senior horticulturist at Laurel Hill, throughout the pandemic, there was a rise in visitors at urban cemeteries: "People found that they needed a place to go…the cemetery was found by many to be a wonderful place to really be able to spread out, safely social distance. To be outside." Since 2020, cemeteries around the country have

offered innovative programming to promote themselves as places of public amusement, sport, and entertainment. Tepper elaborated that the cemetery he stewards offers a movie night on a large screen, historic tours, a fun run, and a charity gala — The Gravedigger's Ball.

So, is love of place about finding hallowed ground in the everyday? Discovering enchantment in the dandelion-strewn alley behind the drycleaners? Planting a garden at the margins of a community park? Reframing our conceptions of this green space — the urban graveyard — not only as a repository of local ghost lore, but as a place for the living to gather, engage in fellowship, bring children to play (respectfully) with their biological, spiritual, or geographic ancestors?

Ellicott City — Local Playground of Ancestors and Children

I fall deeper in love with a small city close to our home every day — Ellicott City, MD. This enduring urban center was founded by three entrepreneurial, philanthropic Quaker brothers in 1772. In 2022, Ellicott City celebrated its 250 year history with events celebrating people who contributed to its thriving, including founding father Charles Carroll, renowned African American scientist and Almanac writer Benjamin Banneker, Principal of the Patapsco Female Institute and science textbook writer Almira Hart Lincoln Phelps, and Mohawk leader Mihšihkinaahkwa (Chief Little Turtle), who experienced an abiding friendship with the Ellicott family. Situated between Washington, DC and Baltimore, MD, Ellicott City — then called 'the hollow' and later, Ellicott's Mills — soon grew from a small mill town to become the seedbed of America's industrial revolution.

In January of 2015, I met my husband Josh at a small tavern at the bottom of the hill in Ellicott City called Cocoa Lane. This day was not only the first time I met Josh, but it was also the first time I met historic, Old Ellicott City. Several months later, Josh would take my father to Cocoa Lane and ask for my hand in marriage. And less than a year later, a flood would devastate Ellicott City, wiping out forever the granite-slabbed-pub where we first shared peanut butter chocolate beers and tacos (gross, but so good). Cocoa Lane would be gone forever, never to be restored.

This was the beginning of a love story. This small city — first stop on the B&O Railroad, birthplace of mechanized milling, early sanctuary of religious tolerance, resilient survivor 16 floods — had become my playground. I have never known Ellicott City without the divisiveness of high stakes local politics. Ellicott City has experienced two 100-year floods in the past seven years alone, opening public

debate about historic preservation, how ongoing development contributes to flooding, environmental sustainability, support for local businesses, restorative justice for historically displaced Black communities, and more.

But division and polarization exist in every city, large and small. Where is the playground amidst the division? If we think back to our own childhoods, if most of us are honest, we will admit that our first experiences with playgrounds were not always happy and carefree. Playground politics dominated, including bullying, isolation, cliques, alliances. These are not invasive species to playgrounds but rather kith and kin.

In *The Flowering Wand: Rewilding the Sacred Masculine*, author Sophie Strand writes:

> *Why does God come among us? The importance is not in the mystical abstraction but in the very tactile reality of our embodiment in a specific time and a specific ecology... When we meditate, let us not ascend, but descend...Ensoulment is ensoilment. Soul is soil.*

While Strand does not identify as a traditional Christian, she is drawn to the earthiness of a God who makes himself flesh to walk humbly — dirtily — among social misfit friends in a particular time and place. Her point is not that Jesus' teachings cannot be relevant for us today, but that if we are to truly cultivate fertile ground in our hearts for the proverbial mustard seed of faith to be planted, we need first to examine how we have removed Jesus from his own cultural, ecological, and mythic root systems. In short, we fall more in love with Christ when we see his Galilee, his remote Northern Palestine, as a playground, fecund with seeds for exploration. Where even the mustard seed — the weed, the invasive species, the small one — is the substance of the Kingdom of God.

The Ellicotts understood this deeply, that to walk humbly with their God was to get in the dirt with their diverse neighbors and play together, to till a soil for all to thrive. The Ellicotts paid for roads, refined their neighbors' first wheat crops for free after convincing them to switch from tobacco for the health of the soil, and gifted city land and local granite to different faith communities to build their own houses of worship. Ellicott City was becoming a playground.

Like many during the pandemic, my husband and I have lived among the living and the dead. We lost our firstborn son, Samuel, to sudden infant death (SIDS) only a year before the first COVID cases were traced in the United States. His death was quickly followed by the birth of Benjamin and 20-months later, our daughter, Phoebe. Benji and Phoebs, as we affectionately call them, were both born premature and medically fragile in a season when those with health concerns were advised to take extreme measures to protect themselves. So, the first years of our babies' lives have been in the liminal space we have all been holding between life and death. And we continue to inhabit that space as we try and often fail to figure out how to incorporate Samuel into our lives on earth, even as he is fully alive and well in the arms of God. So, the cemetery, for reasons that felt particular to us, became our playground during this pandemic season. A place physically representing the now and the not yet.

Only a mile or two outside of Ellicott City's Main Street is a little gem of an oft overlooked, discarded playground — Whipps Garden Cemetery, founded in the 1830s by the Whipps family. It was a local family grave park, not associated with a church. After the last burial in 1915, the cemetery was forgotten and neglected until 1984 when a local civic group, the St. Johns Community Association, committed themselves to the "irresistible urge to put the place in order." And the community, over several decades, restored the garden cemetery into a community gathering place. A playground. The garden park now boasts Bay-Wise Certification through its ecologically friendly gardening practices, historically relevant preserved iron gates and gravestones, and several different garden areas that capture the style of Victorian English Garden. The tombstones of the many children buried at Whipps are dressed in a Maryland state flag.

Ellicott City was more than a birthplace of American innovation, having been founded four years earlier than America herself. For me, it has been the playground of our burgeoning family's love story — from first kiss, to marriage proposal, to the first places we took our newborns out in public, for our earthly children to commune with the children of Ellicott City's past. The comingling of the sacred and profane, the living and the dead, the prolific and mundane, the spoken and unsaid. A playground, a garden, a cemetery, a compost heap. Where the deaths and tragedies of the past — both individual and communal — serve as soil for a still unfolding, playful future.

113

The closing act of Ellicott City's 250th anniversary celebrations occurred in December of 2022. The grand finale was a historic musical called On National Road. A week and a half before Christmas, with the anniversary of our first-born son's passing heavy in the air, we went to the play. It had all the kitsch and camp and awkwardness that one could hope for in local theater. The through line, for me, was the river herself. The signature song, "Patapsco," is a melodic current whose refrain runs through the play: "

> *Hey, River, I'm listenin' / You're young and yet old / Your waters bring life / Let your secrets be told / Come whisper your wisdom / Your song without end / Roll on to great waters, Patapsco.*

The Patapsco is no river of living waters referred to in the Book of Revelation. But her presence has sourced the historic milling economy, the flourishing faith communities, the natural beauty, and has fed the many gardens, including Whipps Garden Cemetery, that whisper of that garden in a city that we all wait for. ✴

FORGIVE AND PLAY

NESS

THE

GROUND

William "Blinky" Rodriguez

Executive Director of Champions In Service, Leadership Foundation of San Fernando and Greater Los Angeles

Seeing the city as God's playground is not for the faint of heart. You get there by traveling on streets strewn with scarred humanity. At least that's my story.

Three days after I buried Sonny, my son, I was driving down Van Nuys Boulevard. A song came on the radio, on one of those "oldies but goodies" stations, KRLA.

...Sunny, thank you for the sunshine you gave
Sunny, thank you for the love you brought my way.
You gave to me your all in all, and now I feel ten feet tall
Sunny, one so true...I love you.

I did not feel ten feet tall. I felt broken. My city felt broken. That was our song, Sonny and me.

Sonny was killed in a drive by shooting while learning to drive a stick shift on Borden Avenue, in Sylmar. In my city, Los Angeles. The City of Angels. The San Fernando Valley, where I call home. He was 16.

My city was a battleground, and I was a broken man driving that day. And the spirit of God told me to go to Pacoima. Pacoima killed my son. And then the spirit said Go.

And I kept driving. I drove up over the tracks on San Fernando Road.

I prayed so violently as I drove, more violently than I ever had before or ever have since. I don't know what people thought about me as I was driving. I was angry. I was a madman. But the Lord said go and so I went.

And the Spirit of God was talking to me as I drove. I felt God telling me to bind up the murder and violence and darkness in this city.

I came to Lehigh Avenue and made a right onto Carl St. As I made my turn, I saw 12–15 young men on the corner under a tree that looked like an umbrella. I stop. I'm watching them. They don't know who I am, and they are watching me as I idle.

This hatred was trying to consume me. I tried to not feed it. It was choking me. I tried to not make war. I tried to listen to God.

As we watched each other, the spirit of God arrested me and told me that the love starts here. Right now. With these young men. Since that day in February 1990, me and my colleagues have dedicated our lives to violence prevention, gang intervention and bringing peace to the street through diversion and development. We choose not to give in to the battleground.

116 About one year after Sonny was murdered, I met his killers. Three young men, who rolled up on my son and shot him. In the courtroom, my wife Lilly and I listen, and the wounds are being reopened inside of me. When we arrived at the courthouse, there were 30 people supporting my son's killers looking at us like we were the ones who had done wrong. My son's grave had been defiled recently. That anger is welling up inside me again. Choking me again. I was having a hard time fulfilling the call of God to love.

I am no stranger to the justice system. Before Sonny was murdered, I had to see my oldest son David be made to look like a beast. I have seen injustice happen. I saw it. I heard it. I chewed on it.

I was right beside David as we navigated the juvenile justice system years before. I held his hand as he was led back to the juvenile hall. The same hand I held when he was seven years old as we walked to an altar call together where he said yes to Jesus. I told him that I would be there with him every step of the way because this justice system is more like a battleground for those who can't afford it. He spent 37 years in Prison with no window in his cell. I had a chance to see justice at its worst.

But we have a choice to make. We can live in battlegrounds, or we can live in playgrounds.

Lilly chose to pray for the families of the young men who killed Sonny. She chose to pray with one of the mothers of the young men who killed my son in the bathroom at the courthouse.

After 3 months of court proceedings, I chose to listen to the call of my God. My God was calling me to forgive the three young men.

In the living room of my home, I said "Lilly, I believe God wants us to forgive the guys that murdered Sonny". She said nothing and walked upstairs. In the morning, she came to me and said "Blinky, I am in agreement with you. I am in agreement to forgive."

And God had his way. I said yes, Lord. Lilly said yes, Lord. We both said yes, Lord. I still say yes, Lord.

We chose to be obedient to the law of mercy rather than the law of sacrifice. I told the District Attorney we wanted the opportunity to forgive Sonny's killers and to ask for leniency for the two young men who were in the car with the trigger man. The DA was not happy. "Back up", I had to tell him. "This is not your business. This is our business. This is what we are going to do. We are going to forgive."

In the courtroom, I walked to the front and looked at Sonny's killer. He would not look at me. "Look at me" I said. "I am talking to you." When he looked at me, I said "I want you to know that we forgive you, man. You may have taken Sonny's life, but you didn't take his soul. You deal with God now as you move forward."

That forgiveness was not my own. I wrestled with it. But God manifested it in me.

I am not the only father that has lost his son to violence. Not by a long shot. I am not unique. Many of the people we now work with have known their cities and communities to be battlegrounds. In fact, they still see them that way. They might as well be crawling on the ground to the front lines. They get down in the wee hours and can get down with taking someone's life. The kid of someone else. People in some of these neighborhoods were stepping over bodies like it was normal. Burying their sons like it was normal. There's nothing normal about burying your son.

Instead, we choose to see a playground where God can work in amazing ways.

These are not just words. This idea of seeing a playground instead of a battleground is a choice to make. This is real. No, it does not often look like children laughing on slides and swings. It often looks more like showing up in the middle of the night after a drive by shooting. Yellow tape. Staying with the wailing mother. Calming the friends who want vengeance. Finding resources for funerals. Being there when the dirt hits the coffin.

There are battlegrounds in our city, full of blood and pain. We cannot ignore that. But here's the deal: we can either give in to it or choose to see a better way.

In our work at Champions In Service, we choose the playground over the battleground. It is long, slow work sometimes. I believe the best is yet to come.

We used to follow helicopters around the city so we could show up at the yellow tape, on the scene of violent crimes to make sure the situation did not escalate. Playing defense instead of offense. Today, we are working across the valley with initiatives ranging from street intervention and violence prevention to re-entry case management with employment assistance, court advocacy, and even pro-bono tattoo removal to increase job opportunities and remove tattoos that symbolized gang affiliation, all because we choose to see our city as a playground. Seeing the city as a playground instead of a battleground allows us the freedom to get creative. It creates an atmosphere where discussions can happen that would never have happened before. In that neighborhood in Pacoima, there is now a Los Angeles Police Department (LAPD) program where 11 cops patrol the neighborhood, not looking to arrest but acting more like mentors. That's a playground mentality.

Donald "Big D" Garcia, was a notorious prison gang leader who was working with me. We began building relationships with some of the gang members in the community. Over time, we got connected. And on October 31, 1993, in a park across from where my son was killed, 76 gang leaders showed up and a truce was negotiated. The Valley Unity Peace Treaty was signed and in the next year, gang-related deaths dropped from 56 to 2 in the Valley. Those meetings continued every Sunday for over a year. That's a playground mentality.

These are the lepers that nobody wants to touch. We must show them that there is hope for them too. In the midst of what could be a battleground, I've seen gang members laughing, smiling. Breaking bread. And the enemy is right there. Leaving one of our events and not being harassed or gaffled up by LAPD. That's playground mentality.

The greatest game I have ever seen in my life was Pacoima vs. San Fernando. We organized this game, all of the cliques of Pacoima vs all of the cliques of San Fernando. The Enchilada Bowl on Super Bowl Weekend at Richie Valens Park. God's power was at work.

In the beginning when Sonny was killed, my sons Gabriel, Donovan and Robert were out for vengeance and hated Pacoima. Hated them. My sons played in that game. There was victory on that field, in that playground. There was victory they can't be matched in my life because my family was spared.

In January 2023, David received a call from Scott Budnick, founder of the Anti-Recidivism Coalition. Scott told David that at his most recent visit to the California State Prison in Lancaster an inmate approached him and asked, "Do you know Blinky Rodriguez?" Scott told the man that he knew me well. "I would like to talk to him," the man said. Scott asked why and the man said, "Because I am the guy who murdered his son."

I wish I could say I was excited. I wish I could say I was ready. I was not. How could anybody be prepared to meet one of their loved one's murderers? But I knew I at least needed to pray about it and be open to the possibility. One of the things I have learned about God's playground is you don't always get to choose who you play with. And then, sure enough, God told me to go and meet this man who had taken my son's life.

On January 30, David and I got in the car and made our way to Lancaster. Scott met us there and escorted me into a room to wait. Suddenly, a man approached. Scott introduced us and this man who murdered my son was within arm's length of me. It had been thirty-three years since I had met this man (at that time no more than a child) in the courtroom at his trial where he looked at me with such disdain. This time he looked at me and asked, "Can I get a hug?" By the grace of God, I grabbed him, embraced him, and we sobbed together like two little babies. For the next two and a half hours we sat together in that chapel in the state prison and began to witness God healing not just him and not just me, but both of us.

The Bible says that when one soul comes to the Kingdom of God, the angels in heaven rejoice. On that day, the angels in heaven threw a party.

But they that wait upon the Lord shall renew their strength; they shall mount up with wings as eagles; they shall run, and not be weary; and they shall walk, and not faint. —Isaiah 40:31⚽

〜〜〜〜〜〜〜〜〜〜〜〜〜〜〜〜〜〜

DR. DAVE HILLIS

DR. MARK LABBERTON

Former President of
Fuller Theological Seminary

In Conversation

Dave: We've been exploring this idea of seeing the city as a playground, rather than a battleground. How does that metaphor sit with you?

Mark: It's a very evocative image. It has all kinds of positive implications and raises a lot of suggestive questions as well. What I love about it, is that it changes the nature of the intensity. It moves from the anxiety and tightness of war (which cities can feel like) to a much more relaxed, playful, curious, vulnerable, fully present vision; all in real time. It's not ever about the past or future, only the moment. It's a potentially constructive and helpful image because of this immediacy, creating the possibility of play where you're just simply giving yourself to the moment, the apparatus, the social exchanges—all that arises in play. This does involve a lot of interesting things, depending on the nature of the playground, the other players, and the wider context, too.

On the literal playground, much of the play is individual. You're playing in parallel, with or next to others, not in competition. Individual play is partly what allows it to feel so free and easy because it's not demanding that my neighbor-player is interested in doing what I'm interested in doing. And I'm not hampered by what they're doing. Fundamentally, it's free play and part of its joy is that you do get to just explore the concept within your own imagination. I love all that. And as a metaphor, that freedom for creativity and lack of competition allows us to see a new way of living, neighboring, and working in cities. On the playground, there is also negotiated space, and when there is conflict that we have to negotiate, it can be lighter because the nature of the playground is non-competitive. To be able to see and engage life has been shown by considerable research to have very positive benefits, including the chance to demonstrate and experience our humanity in such important ways.

D: Absolutely. You know, one interesting book for me has been "Man At Play" by Hugo Rahner. He argues that there's nothing on God's "job description" that necessitated creation. God was free to do whatever God wanted to do, and if God didn't want to create, God didn't have to create it. So, he then asks, why did God? And his answer is God's playfulness. I just had never thought about it quite in that way before.

122

M: Yes, that is interesting. A very close friend of mine is a child development specialist, and he has talked about how much play is a part of our learning and becoming a person. Play is essential developmentally. So, in one sense, of course, we grow out of playgrounds. Which is an interesting idea to play with in this idea of city as playground. Why do we grow out of playgrounds? Well, our body sizes change. That's part of it. Our developmental work brings us to a place where the childhood playground is no longer what it once was to us, and we have other "playgrounds" to which we move. It's important for us to think about what is the nature of the playground and the play that we're describing as the city. In addition, what does it mean to have a mindfulness of different playgrounds for different chapters, and different seasons, different players, and different cities.

D: Yes, and the importance of play, as a generator of fun and joy and laughter, but also play that sparks imagination, innovation, creativity, is so important in these times. Part of what we're trying to work out with a lot of our colleagues who want to make a positive change in the city socially and spiritually is that part of our problem is we just can't get out of our own way. We take things so damn seriously. I wondered if we would all be helped by looking at our work in a bit more of a playful perspective.

M: I think you are getting at one of the things plaguing our society right now. Everything seems so intense. Everything seems wrong. Everything seems like it's dire and urgent. So that tends to squeeze out the freedom of play and the ability for lighthearted activities and conversations. So, part of the polarity around political conversations right now is it literally seems impossible to even imagine something that is not the reality that you are committed to defending. That's a totally different energy than the energy that would release somebody in the abandonment of play. So, I think what you're onto here is significant, especially because of the way that it reflects back, at the current moment, the impossibility of play.

A footnote here is the gaming industry. Games have always been full of competition and rivalry, but now in the vast electronic playground of gaming competitors are endlessly involved in killing. To win involves lots of skills, but killing is now at the heart of such "play." This is such a significant shift. By contrast, the ordinary wins and losses of playground competition become all the more important.

D: What does that metaphorical playground look like to you?

M: Just yesterday I was walking along the street that I often walk. There's an AA group that meets late in the afternoon almost every day. As I was passing, this guy driving a Silver Shadow Rolls Royce pulled up, parked, and walked into this group. Now, if you saw the group that I normally see when I walk along that street, they are not driving that model car. I was thinking that this is such an interesting example of what a playground can be. Anybody gets to walk into that room and once they're in the room and they're talking about the issues of their life, everyone is on equal ground. The only affirmation is, "I'm an alcoholic." Everything else about their lives could be completely, totally different. So that's the great equalizer of a playground. Now, that playground image has limits, of course. To think about the image of city as playground, it needs to flourish at the core of what it is and then have an integrated account of how the playground fits everything else that the city also is, which can look like a battleground with anguish, suffering and poverty.

So what does that image of the playground suggest? It brings freedom, it brings the richness of what I would call a theology of play, it brings an ease that is not about conformity, not about rule following, it's not fundamentally about competition. It's just that everybody gets to play. And we need spaces like that, especially with people that are unlike us, in order to somehow come closer to each other than we might ever otherwise be.

D: I love that. I think that's part of what we're hoping the idea of seeing the city as a playground does. We're hoping it becomes that North Star of sorts that doesn't gloss over these hard places, the battleground places, but that somehow gives us an inspiration for enduring it, for being able to work through it.

M: Yeah, I think that's right. I also thought about the museums. Some museums more than others, but there are plenty of museums that feel very much like a playground, and where a person has literally played at their art in the best sense. It's now in a context where all kinds of people come for all sorts of reasons to experience that playground. That kind of playground spawns other playgrounds.

D: That's a great example because it's not transactional. And whatever else a playground is, while there may be some negotiation, it ceases to be transactional. Even when we can't articulate it, we feel it. Another piece of this project is in thinking about metaphors themselves. One of my working hypotheses is that to be human is to be metaphorical. And the only way we can make sense of the meaning of life is through metaphor. However, I think most of the time, they are unconscious metaphors. I've thought often that a lot of the anger and violence in these times is the result of these unexamined metaphors running into each other.

M: Metaphor has been a huge part of both my life of faith but also my academic life because so much of what I've been most interested in is how people come to claims of knowledge about God. And so much of that has to do with how we handle metaphors, because it's one of our only ways of accessing and comprehending something that we may be talking about. I have been working with some colleagues on a project, *Rethinking Church in the 21st Century.* One of the things that we're working on is trying to distill the metaphors that have gotten lost, diminished, betrayed about the foundations of the Christian faith. What does it mean to positively, non-defensively, recultivate, reexamine metaphors that feel as though they have gotten lost at a very high price? What about yeast? What about light? What about clay jars? These important ideas have been replaced with images of public and visible power, a competition for a powerful public stage, ideologically defined. It's a failure of imagination. It feels very much like we have a poverty of imagination, a poverty of metaphors about the nature of the church. And, and if you adopt a skewed list of metaphors, and then you say the church must be that metaphor, then you've lost so much of what I think Jesus subversively wants to give us.

One of the things I find attractive about metaphors is that they leave space for mystery, surprise, humility, and they also make way for more of a both/and world, rather than either/or world. So, the richness does not corner me or leave me frozen, nor does it do those things to my neighbors.

D: I think that's so important. Thomas Merton would say that contradiction is actually not a negative, but a positive. And sometimes we find God in the contradiction. Part of the power of metaphor, I think, is that it allows for contradiction to exist. And, I think we need that. It moves us away from that kind of false dichotomy of this or that. Seeing the city as a playground is certainly not the only metaphor that someone could use, but what I like about it is that it doesn't corner us. It just points in a direction.

M: Yes. It is not at all reductionistic; it's amplifying of some elements that are really critical. It doesn't make all-inclusive claims, it's not totalizing, but rather momentary and partial. To hold the metaphor itself as a form of play, holding playgrounds as a form of play rather than as something exhaustive or exclusive. ⚽

128

Now, go play.

130

www.ingramcontent.com/pod-product-compliance
Lightning Source LLC
Chambersburg PA
CBHW042335030426
42335CB00028B/3357